ALVIN CORBYN

The Modern Collector

How to Start and Grow a Unique Collection

This book was professionally typeset on Reedsy.
Find out more at reedsy.com

Contents

Introduction: Why Collecting Matters

There's something pretty fantastic about collecting, don't you think? Whether it's a shelf full of old vinyl records or a box packed with postcards from another era or your favorite action figures which you didn't unbox, a collection tells a story—not just about the stuff, but about the person who put it together!

Think about it... Have you ever saved something like a concert ticket from a favorite band or a cool old coin you found at a flea market and thought, "This is special"? Well if you have, You're definitely not the only one. Collecting isn't just about having and storing things—it's about the feelings and stories attached to them, the memories they bring back, and the satisfaction of finding that perfect addition to your growing stash.

But why do we invest so much to collect in the first place?

For many, it's all about nostalgia. That collection of baseball cards you started as a kid might bring back memories of weekends with your dad, sitting around the kitchen table, opening new packs, and hoping for a rare card. Or that collection of Pokemon cards you used swap with your friends during lunchtime at school. To others, collecting is like a treasure hunt— tracking down rare items, making smart trades, and watching the value of your collection grow. Whether it's about the emotions, the thrill of the hunt, or even the hope for potential payday, chasing after a collection gives us a thrill of adventure, sense of purpose, and accomplishment.

But collecting's more than just gathering stuff to look at in the future. Every collection has a story behind it! It's about passion, curiosity, and the excitement of learning everything you can about your favorite items, whether it's vintage toys, cards, rare stamps, or first-edition books.

Here's the greatest thing: anyone can be a collector! You don't need to be some millionaire bidding at fancy auctions. In fact, some of the world's coolest collections started small—like picking up a seashell on a family beach trip or finding a quirky item at a thrift store. Every collection starts somewhere, and that's the beauty of it!

In this book, we'll take a deep dive into the classic hobby of collecting. Whether you're just starting out or have been at it for years, there's always more to learn in the art. We'll talk about why people collect, help you figure out what might be worth collecting (if you don't already have something in mind), and give you practical tips for growing and taking care of your collection.

By the time you finish reading, you'll have a solid road map for getting started, locating and valuing your items, and even organizing and showing off your collection proudly. We'll also explore the wide world of collecting—from people who turned their hobby into a career to legendary collectors with famous (and sometimes super odd!) collections.

So, let's jump in. Who knows? Your next great find might be just around the corner.

Chapter 1: Choosing Your Collection Focus

Starting a collection can feel like embarking on an exciting treasure hunt. But before you dive into it, you'll need to figure out what you want to collect. In the world full of collectibles, it might seem overwhelming and confusing at first, but choosing a proper focus for your collection is part of the fun. This chapter will guide you through finding your passion, narrowing your choice, and starting the journey to start your collection with confidence.

1.1 Discover Your Passion

Do start a proper collection you have look inside yourself and tap your passion or love for something. Without clear passion, a collection is nothing but a box full of strange and unused things up in your attic. Every great collection starts with just a simple spark. What makes you stop and take a second look? Maybe it's vintage comic books, rare coins, first edition books or something completely unexpected, like antique teapots or spoons. The key is to think about what naturally draws you in and keeps you engaged that you forget how much time you spent on it. Do you have a soft spot for history, rare books, love all things pop culture, or find yourself fascinated by nature?

Think back to the moments when you've been excited about something— what did that feel like? Maybe you've always gravitated toward artwork or you can't ignored an old vinyl record without thumbing through the pile. Your passion is your compass; follow it and see where it leads you...

Nostalgia has a funny way of sparking a collection. Sometimes, it only takes one glance at something from your past, and suddenly, you're flooded with memories. Maybe it's that action figure you played with every day or the dolls that lined your bedroom shelf. Or perhaps it's the sound of a classic video game startup screen that brings back the thrill of mastering a mission for the first time.

Imagine the thrill and joy of revisiting those old toys or games as part of a collection. Each item feeling like a time machine, taking you back to those carefree days when all you worried about was which level to beat next or what adventure you and your toys would go on. It's not just about owning the stuff; it's about reliving the emotions and experiences tied to them.

For example, I have a friend who started collecting old video game cartridges after finding his childhood console in a box at his old house. What started as a bit of nostalgia quickly grew into a full-blown hobby! Every time he adds a new game to his collection, it's like stepping back into the days of sitting cross-legged on the floor, controller in hand, determined to beat the boss level. His collection isn't just about the games—it's about reliving the thrills and fun of his teenage days.

Not sure where to start? Sometimes, all you need is a little spark of inspiration. Going through your old stuffs, stepping into a museum, wandering through an antique shop, or visit a collector's gathering—you never know what might catch your imagination. Seeing someone else's collection up close can be like opening a door to a whole new world. Maybe you stroll through a photography exhibit or a yard sale and suddenly find yourself fascinated by the displays. Or you stop at a booth filled with old postcards and realize you've always been drawn to the stories behind them.

The world is filled with fascinating objects, each with its own history and charm. Sometimes, all it takes is a moment of inspiration, and you'll find yourself drawn to it. Keep your eyes open—you might stumble upon something that hooks you up in the most unexpected places. That's the beauty of collecting, which has been cherished by people for centuries.

1.2 Narrowing Down Your Options

When you first dip your toes into the ocean of collecting, it's might feel like a kid in a candy store—everything looks exciting, and you might be tempted to grab a little bit of everything. But hold on! Instead of getting overwhelmed by the endless options, it's smarter (and more fun!) to start small. Think of it like picking a lane. Focus on a specific niche or theme within a larger category, and delve into in, so your collection gets direction and purpose.

For example, if the engravings or shape of coins catch your eye, don't try to collect every coin ever minted—hone in on coins from a certain country or a particular era first, and then move on. This way, your collection will feel more attainable and meaningful, and each addition will bring a sense of accomplishment rather than confusion. On top of that, it's easier to track down items when you know exactly what you're going after. As your collection increases, you can always expand to broader horizons later on.

Before you rush headfirst into collecting, it's better to do some digging.

- How easy—or difficult—is it to find what you want to collect?
- Where can you find it to get started?
- What is the best process to preserve your collection?

Some items, like baseball cards or stamps, are super popular and quite easy to come by, while others, like 18th-century furniture or news papers or rare fossils, might take more time (and money) to track down and keep intact. There's no right or wrong choice here—it's all about what keeps you hyped. Just keep in mind that rare items can be pricier and require more patience to get, while common items like playing cards, books or vinyl records etc. are easier to find but might not have the same thrill of the hunt. Either way, a bit of research can help you set realistic expectations and figure out how to best start setting up your collection.

Also, creating your own set of rules for building your collection is like road map—it helps you stay focused and makes the whole journey more rewarding. Start by finding out what truly matters to you. Are you hunting for rare treasures that could increase in value over time, or are you more interested in pieces that tug at your heartstrings? Maybe you're on a budget and want to keep your finds affordable, setting a price cap so you don't break the bank.

You might also prefer the rush of discovering local items—at flea markets, thrift stores, antique shops or garage sales—rather than scouring online listings or traveling far and wide. Whatever your criteria, setting some regulations will make your collection feel more intentional, meaningful, and uniquely yours. It's like planning your own personal treasure hunt!

1.3 Balancing Passion with Practicality

For many collectors, the heart of their collection is an emotional attachment to the items they collect. Maybe it's something that connects you to your childhood, or perhaps you just love the beauty or history behind what you collect. On the contrary, some people collect with the idea that their collection could be an investment, with certain items appreciating in value over time.

Confusion between emotional connection and financial profitability while collections is the most challenging task for beginner collectors. It's important to strike a balance between these two approaches. Collect what you love first and foremost, but it doesn't hurt to keep an eye on things with future value if that's something that interests you.

When you're looking at items to collect, it's wise to consider whether they might increase in financial value down the road. For example, retro video game consoles have seen a huge rise in value over the last decade, and first-edition books can become extremely valuable if they're rare enough or the author was notable. Think about if there's demand for the item and whether it has cultural or historical significance.

While no one knows the future, a little research can help you make educated guesses about what might become a collector's gem.

1.4 Collections with a Story

Every collection tells a story. It's not just about the objects; it's about the journey taken to obtain them. Consider how your collection reflects who you are, what you're passionate about, or the memories you hold dear. If you collect antique cameras, for example, each one might represent a different chapter in the history of photography, as well as your own journey in discovering these relics.

A great way to make your collection stand out is by creating a theme. This doesn't mean your collection has to be narrow—it just needs to be cohesive. If you're collecting vintage cameras, for instance, you could focus on a particular brand or time period, building a narrative around how photography has evolved over time. It'll also help enhance the experience visitors of your collection, should you decide to display your collection in any time.

A strong and interesting theme can make your collection more meaningful and enjoyable to share with others. It might make your journey to collecting more exciting too.

1.5 Looking Ahead: Is This Collection Sustainable?

One important thing to consider while starting a collection is whether your chosen collectibles will hold your interest over time. Will you still be excited about it a few years from now? Are there enough items out there to keep you engaged in the adventure? Some collectors burn out because they don't plan for the long term and end up with a collection that feels complete too easy too soon.

Take a moment to think about whether your collection will continue to inspire you in the future.

Practical considerations matter, too. Does your collection need a lot of space? Some collections, like vintage cars or large art pieces, require dedicated storage, while others, like stamps or coins, can be neatly organized in small albums but they need proper care as they are very delicate due to their age. Think about how much room you have and what kind of care your items will need as your collection grows.

1.6 Taking the First Step...

By now you've finally figured out what you want to collect—now comes the fun part! The key to getting started is simple: just get started. You don't have to wait around for the "perfect" item to come along. Head to a flea market, browse through your local antique shop, or jump online to see what catches your eye.

The most important thing is to make that first purchase with confidence and excitement. It might be a small find, but every great collection starts with just one item. Who knows? That first piece could end up being the cornerstone of something amazing!

Chapter 2: Getting Started with Your First Collection

Alright, you've decided to become a collector. Whether it's vintage postcards, antique vases, or classic vinyl records, collecting is an exciting and deeply personal adventure. The great thing about collecting is that it's a journey— one that doesn't need to be rushed. We"ll take this one step at a time.

2.1 Starting Small

Every collection needs starts somewhere. It's easy to get carried away and want to scoop up everything in sight, trying go everywhere and create chaos, but the best collections are built thoughtfully and slowly. Begin with just a few items that interest you and spark genuine excitement. Think of it as dipping your toes in the water before jumping into the deep end. Starting small lets you get a feel for the process and understand your tastes without being overwhelmed by too many choices or costs.

Imagine your collection as a puzzle. You don't need all the pieces at once; you need to go piece by piece and sometimes, finding those missing parts is the best part of the journey. With each new addition, you'll feel the satisfaction of seeing the bigger picture slowly come together!

Gathering a collection is a marathon, not a sprint. There's no rush to fill every shelf or box with new finds. In fact, half the fun is in the waiting, searching, researching, and stumbling upon that perfect addition when you expect it the least. Think of it like growing a garden. You plant a few seeds, nurture them, and watch them bloom over time. The same goes for collecting. Patience makes the process all the more rewarding.

Take your time, enjoy the hunt, and let your collection grow naturally. You're building something meaningful, not just pile up things.

2.2 Where to Find Collectibles

One of the most exciting aspect of collecting is the thrill of the search. And sometimes, the best treasures are hiding right under your nose, while you've been looking at online listings, social media or advertisement. Flea markets, garage sales, thrift stores, and estate sales can be gold mines for hidden collectibles. There's something excitement about stumbling upon a rare find that someone else might have overlooked. Plus, there's nothing like the feeling of walking away with a great deal on a valuable piece. Also that feeling of satisfaction of knowing the value of something which others might not is worth it!

Exploring local spots is also part of the adventure. Every trip to a flea market or thrift shop can be an opportunity to discover something new, and that sense of uncovering is what keeps the experience intact and fun.

Inevitably, we live in the digital age, and the internet opens up a whole new world of possibilities, we are the one click away from getting our hands on the desired collectible. Websites like eBay, Etsy, and Craigslist are treasure troves for collectors of all niches. Whether you're looking for vintage toys or rare coins, you can find almost anything with a few clicks. But beware—online marketplaces can be tricky and dangerous! Make sure you're buying from authentic sellers, read reviews, and take your time to avoid falling into scams.

If you're ready to dive deeper and feel the essence of professionalism in your collector's journey, auctions and conventions are perfect places to find high-quality or rare items. These events bring together like-minded collectors and often feature pieces you won't find anywhere else. But don't go in unprepared. Do your homework before attending. Research the items up for sale, know their market value, and most importantly, set a spending limit. Otherwise, you'll be ripped apart by those intellectuals with years of experience and knowledge.

These events can be fast-paced and competitive, but with a little preparation and research, you can walk away with something truly special.

There's a saying: "It's not what you know, but who you know!" This is true in the world of collecting, too. Joining forums, social media groups, newsletters or local collector clubs can open doors to new sources of information and trades. Networking with fellow collectors helps you gain valuable advice and build connections that will enrich your collection.

Sometimes, the best finds come through word-of-mouth recommendations or trades with other like-minded enthusiasts.

2.3 Evaluating Quality

When it comes to collectibles, quality is everything. Whether you're eyeing a vintage comic book or a classic vinyl record, condition can be the difference between a prized gem and a dud. But what exactly should you look for? It depends on what you're collecting. A coin in pristine, mint condition will shine much brighter—both in value and appeal—than one that's been scuffed or handled. For action figures or toys, original packaging that's still intact could skyrocket the item's worth. Each collectible has its own set of rules and guidelines to determine its value, but there are a few things to always keep in mind: check for signs of age, wear, ensure authenticity, and confirm that the item is complete.

Think of it like shopping for a car. Whether it's a gleaming sports car fresh off the lot or a rare vintage model, condition is the ultimate deciding factor. A few scratches here and there might not be a dealbreaker, but they certainly lower the value.

However, if you only want the piece for its emotional value, then the condition matter the least in t

Chapter 3: Growing and Expanding Your Collection

Building a worthwhile collection is about more than just gathering items you see here and there. It requires careful thought, strategy, and passion. This chapter will explore how you can expand your collection with intention, master the market, and build relationships that can enhance not only your collection's value but also your expertise and fun as a beginning modern collector.

3.1 Developing a Unique Collection Strategy

As your collection starts to get bigger, it's important to think about the direction in which you want to grow. Many collectors get sucked into the blackhole of adding items randomly, which can result in a cluttered and scrambled collection. To truly collect professionally with purpose, you need a full proof strategy that will help you refine your focus and make smarter collections.

First and foremost, Stop! Take a step back and look at what you've collected till now as a whole. Ask yourself: What's missing? What stories do you want your collection to tell? Constructing a vision for your collection can be the definitive difference between merely accumulating objects and establishing something truly remarkable. Whether you want to zero in on a particular time period, a specific style, or even rare or obscure subcategories, having this vision will guide your future purchases and bring clarity to your collecting journey.

Additionally, when you continue to find new items, it's important to prioritize quality over quantity. Some of the most respected collections are built not on sheer numbers but on the caliber of the pieces. Fewer, high-quality items often have more impact than a larger, less curated collection. With patience and determination, you can elevate your collection's significance and, ultimately, its value.

3.2 Spotting and Capitalizing on Market Trends

Collecting isn't just about passion—it's also about staying sharp and knowing when to jump in. The value of collectibles can shift rapidly with trends, cultural changes, or even unexpected social or political events. One day, an item might seem ordinary, and the next, it's the most sought-after piece in the collectors market. To enhance your collection wisely, it's crucial to be informed with these trends and be ready to seize the opportunities.

Staying up-to-date can give you a huge advantage. Sometimes, a forgotten collectible gains new attention because of a cultural event—like a popular TV show or an anniversary celebration—making it suddenly valuable. For example, after the release of a new superhero movie, interest in vintage comic books featuring that character might suddenly spike. Or think about retro video games—once considered outdated, many are now highly sought-after as nostalgia kicks in and demand for early editions grows. If you're tuned in to what's happening both in the collector's world and the broader culture, you can catch these shifts before prices rise dramatically. Whether it's rare vinyl records or limited-edition sneakers, staying aware of these trends helps you get ahead of the curve.

Timing is key. Knowing when to buy and when to hold off can make all the difference. During periods when certain items are undervalued or overlooked, you can make smart purchases and hold onto them until demand increases. These small investments can turn into big gains when interest surges.

Of course, the market is always unpredictable, so it's important to balance excitement with careful planning. You're collecting because you love it not because you want to earn profits, but keeping an eye on trends adds an extra layer of fun and excitement.

3.3 Building a Network of Trusted Collectors and Sellers

One of the most rewarding aspects of collecting is the community that you access. While it might seem like a solo mission when you start out, connecting with other collectors and sellers can open doors you never knew existed. These relationships can provide access to rare items, valuable knowledge, and opportunities that often aren't available through mainstream channels.

Building relationships within niche communities is key to this process. Imagine you're searching for a specific limited-edition item, like a rare action figure or a signed first-edition book. Often, fellow collectors have leads on where to find such treasures or may be willing to trade something you need for an item they're looking for which you might posess. Online forums, social media groups, and specialized marketplaces are great places to connect. For example, many collectors have found success joining Facebook groups dedicated to vintage toys or vinyl records, where members share tips, sell items, and trade collection stories to inspire new collectors. These communities can also help you avoid common pitfalls—like overpaying for an item or accidentally buying a fake—by sharing their experiences and advice.

Attending collectors conventions, trade shows, or collector meetups takes this networking to the next level. These events are not just about buying or selling; they're about learning and building relationships. You might meet sellers or enthusiasts who specialize in items you didn't even know existed or strike up a conversation with a fellow collector who points you toward a hidden gem. For example, comic book collectors at conventions often stumble upon rare variants that aren't listed online, or they can get insider knowledge about upcoming releases that will affect the value of certain items. Being able to inspect items in person, talk directly to sellers, and negotiate on the spot gives you a significant advantage over buying solely online.

Moreover, developing long-term relationships with trusted sellers can lead to perks that go beyond a single purchase. Regularly buying from the same vendor, whether it's at a local flea market or an online shop, can make you one of their preferred customers. This might mean first dibs on new inventory or access to exclusive deals before they go public. Some collectors even build such strong relationships with sellers that they're contacted directly when the seller comes across items they know will be of interest.

In the world of collecting, it's often who you know that makes all the difference. By joining a network of collectors and sellers, you'll gain access to opportunities and treasures for your collection that most people never see.

3.4 Mastering the Art of Trading and Negotiation

As your collecting journey continues on, trading and exchanging becomes an increasingly important weapon for the hunt of new items without always having to spend money for collectibles. Successful trading, however, is more art than science! It involves building trust, knowing the right value of your items, and recognizing fair deals when they come up.

When it comes to trading with other collectors, it's essential to approach each deal with mutual respect and transparency. Trading can be a win-win scenario for both scenario, but only if both parties feel they're getting something of equal or greater value for their respective collection. Before entering any trade, do your homework, plan your approach. Understand the rarity and current market value of both the item you'll be exchanging and the one you're interested in acquiring.

Negotiation is also a crucial skill, not just in trades but also in purchases. Whether you're dealing with other collectors, haggling at a flea market, or with a professional item seller, knowing how to negotiate successfully can save you money and help you secure better deals. The key is to stay alert for offers and never rush into decisions. Developing a confident but respectful negotiating style will serve you well in any collecting situation.

3.5 Curating and Letting Go: When Less is More

When your collection is growing steadily, you'll eventually reach a point where curating becomes essential—deciding which items truly enhance the overall theme of your collection and which ones no longer fit. Curating isn't a one-time task; it's an ongoing process of refinement that keeps your collection focused and meaningful. It's about preserving the excitement that led you to start collecting in the first place, while also making room for new, more valuable additions.

For example, say you collect vintage cameras, and over time, you've accumulated dozens from different eras. As your knowledge and taste evolve, you might realize that your real passion lies in one specific brand or time period. At that point, it's worth considering letting go of the outliers that don't align with your core focus. This process of narrowing down ensures that every piece in your collection serves a purpose and contributes to the overall story you want it to tell.

Letting go of items can be hard, especially if they carry sentimental value or if they were once a prized part of your collection. Maybe you've held onto a vintage toy from your childhood that no longer fits with the rest of your passionately curated collection of high-end, limited-edition action figures. While it might be difficult to part with it, selling or trading such pieces can free up space—both physically and mentally—for more significant collectibles. It also gives you the financial freedom to invest in those rare or higher-quality pieces that will elevate your collection higher.

Additionally, consider the potential benefits of selling during a peak market. For instance, if a particular item you own has suddenly gained popularity due to a pop culture event, it might be the perfect time to sell it for a higher price. By doing so, you can fund your future purchases and ensure your collection stays unique and focused on what excites you the most.

A curated collection doesn't just reflect your interests; it tells a story. The careful balance of adding and removing items will result in a collection that feels cohesive, purposeful, and deeply personal. With the passage of time, it will represent not just a collection of objects, but a reflection of your journey as a passionate collector—one that grows and evolves along with your tastes and expertise.

3.6 Becoming a True Expert in Your Niche

Every serious collector eventually reaches a stage where they want to go beyond simply acquiring items—they want to truly master their niche. Gaining expertise can enhance your collection from a personal passion into something extraordinary, filled with meaningful and valuable pieces that only another informed eye would recognize.

Take, for example, a collector of antique watches. At first, they may focus on renowned brands, but over time, a deeper understanding of the history and craftsmanship behind these pieces can open up new avenues of collecting. Learning how different watchmakers innovated over the years or the unique features of certain models can help identify watches that are undervalued but historically significant. Researching these nuances can lead to finding rare gems that others without knowledge might overlook.

Immersing yourself in research—whether through books, documentaries, online resources, or conversations with fellow collectors—sharpens your skills to spot genuine items and avoid duplicates. For instance, vintage sneaker collectors often invest in detailed guides and studies about specific models and collaborations with legendary famous players. This data helps them tell the difference between an original pair and a well-made replica, allowing them to make better-informed decisions when buying or selling.

Another advantage of becoming an expert is being able to recognize trends before they fully take over. If you specialize in a specific area—like 1960s science fiction memorabilia or mid-century modern furniture—your expertise will allow you to predict which items might become more valuable as interest in certain eras or styles rises. Collectors who master their niche also become go-to sources in that niche within their community. For example, a rare coin collector might build such deep knowledge about the history of coins or their backgrounds that others in the community might come to them for advice or for trading rare pieces of coin, giving them exclusive access to coveted items.

3.7 Building Relationships with Sellers for Long-Term Enhancement

To grow your collection strategically, it's not just about what you buy, but from whom you buy. Developing long-term relationships with trusted sellers can be a game-changer. Sellers who know and trust you often provide access to higher-quality items and give you first dibs on new inventory, saving you time and effort in your search.

Imagine you're a vinyl record collector who frequents the same local shop every weekend. Over time, the shop owner gets to know your tastes and lets you know when rare albums that fit your collection come in, or they might even hold items aside for you before listing them for general sale. This insider access often leads to you accessing rare finds that others miss. In the online world, consistent interaction with sellers on auction sites or niche marketplaces can also pay off, with sellers offering discounts or special deals or inside information of exclusive shipment to loyal customers.

These relationships are built on trust and mutual benefit. You might come across sellers at flea markets, antique shops, or even online communities who can offer better prices, knowing you'll return for more business. Sellers are often more willing to negotiate with familiar buyers, particularly on high-value or rare items. For example, a collector of vintage posters might visit the same dealer year after year, gaining both trust and access to posters that never make it to public auctions.

To build these connections, always approach sellers with respect and professionalism. Whether you're negotiating prices at a local market or asking questions about an item online, treating sellers fairly and cordially empowers goodwill. You never know when that rapport will pay off in the form of an exclusive deal or an early tip-off on a rare item you've been hunting for so long.

In short, the relationships you build with sellers can become one of your most valuable resources. These connections can lead to insider opportunities, special discounts, and access to inventory that others may never see, allowing your collection to grow in ways that would be impossible otherwise.

These strategies, you'll not only expand your collection but also enrich your experience as an aspiring collector. Your collection will reflect both your personal growth as a collector and the knowledge you've gained, making it far more valuable and meaningful than a mere assortment of objects.

Chapter 4: Organizing, Displaying, and Caring for Your Collection

For many collectors, the joy of building a collection goes beyond simply acquiring items. It's about caring for those pieces, making them accessible, and presenting them in a way that enhances their value—both personal and, in some cases, monetary. Now, we'll dive into why organizing, displaying, and maintaining your collection matters. We'll also explore practical strategies to help you enjoy your collection more fully while ensuring its preservation for years to come.

4.1 The Power of Organization: Enhancing Your Collecting Experience

Imagine this: you've been collecting vintage postcards for years. One day, you come across a particularly rare postcard online that would be the crown jewel of your collection. You buy it, and when it arrives, you want to compare it with another postcard from a similar era. But you can't find it. Your collection, once a source of pride, has turned into a source of frustration because you didn't have a organization system in place.

Organization isn't just about keeping order—it's about creating more fun and excitement in your collecting journey. When everything is in its designated place, you can find specific items with ease, cherish them more often, and, ultimately, get more worth from your collection. Organized collections offer a sense of accomplishment and provide a much-needed structure to what can easily become chaotic.

As collections increase, chaos can creep in unnoticed. A friend of mine once started collecting antique cameras. At first, he only had a few, so he casually stored them on bookshelves and side tables. But soon, his collection grew— half of it scattered across different rooms. He had no idea where his original Polaroid camera was, and several cameras sustained damage from being poorly stored and without keeping it protected.

This is a common pitfall for collectors. Without proper set up, your most dear collected things get lost, damaged, or even forgotten at a corner at your place. Organization can help you avoid these frustrations and confusions, and once you have a planned method in place, managing your collection becomes your habit and remember, it's not a chore, it's what you love!

4.2 Practical Strategies for Organizing Your Collection

One of the best ways to stay on top of your collection is to catalog it. It is the backbone of organizing your collection. Cataloging not only helps you track what you own but also gives you a deeper understanding of your collection's value and history. Some collectors still love the simplicity of writing everything down in a notebook. Others prefer the precision of spreadsheets where they can list details like the item's origin, condition, and value.

But if you're more tech-savvy, there are plenty of digital tools available, from mobile apps specifically designed for collectors to cloud-based systems that allow you to upload images and keep detailed notes. A vintage toy collector I know uses an app where he stores photos of each item, noting its current condition and any price appreciation over time. Having everything digitized gives him instant access and peace of mind knowing that he can manage and be close to his collection even while traveling or attending auctions or in a break from work.

Your collection, no matter the size, has a story behind them. Grouping each item by theme, era, or category can help create that narrative. For instance, a stamp collector might organize by country of origin, while someone collecting vintage clothing may separate by decade.

A great example of this is a collector who collects travel souvenirs. Instead of lumping everything together, he organizes each item by region—Asia, Europe,

Africa—and within each region, she arranges the items chronologically and country-wise. The outcome? A visual journey through the memories of his travels. When guests come over, he takes them through his adventures, not just showing them items but immersing them with the stories behind them.

Now, Storage is an essential part of maintaining a collection, and different collections require different solutions. Small items like stamps, coins, or baseball cards etc. may need binders with protective sleeves, while larger items like sculptures or antique furniture may require custom shelves or display cases.

I recently visited a collector who specialized in vintage LP records. His solution? A combination of functional and stylish storage. He used record shelving with dividers, but also kept some of his most valuable records on display in protective frames. His collection wasn't just stored; it showed his dedication for his collection and it was showcased in a way that displayed both its beauty and accessibility.

4.3 Creative Display Ideas: Showcasing Your Collection with Pride

Once your collection is organized and safely stored, it's time to think about how to display them. Displaying your collection is not just about showing off—it's about the joy it brings you when you look at them. Take, for instance, someone who collects vintage cameras. They could line them up on a plain shelf, but why not take it a step further? Consider using custom shelving that allows the cameras to be arranged by brand or era, with small placards that tell the story of each piece and background behind collecting it.

One collector I know showcased his collection of historical figurines in a glass cabinet with LED lighting. Each figure has its own place, and the lighting adds a museum-like touch. These small adjustments can turn your collection into an enjoyable art piece that sparks conversations and reflects your personality.

Additionally, It's important to strike a balance between making your collection aesthetically pleasing and keeping it accessible. A display that looks beautiful but is difficult to interact with will only frustrate you in the long run when you want sit and enjoy your collection on a lazy afternoon! For example, vinyl record collectors often display their favorite or rarest albums on the wall, but keep the rest of their collection in easily accessible shelving units.

An antique furniture collector I heard about had a clever setup! The most fragile and valuable pieces were protected behind tampered glass, while the more durable ones were left out for everyday use. This not only safeguarded the most delicate items but also allowed him to enjoy the more robust ones in daily life.

The way you display your collection can convey the story attached to them. Consider the idea of grouping your items in a way that reflects your collection journey or a particular theme. For instance, a travel enthusiast who collects postcards could arrange them geographically or based on special event they were issued, showing a journey from one country to the next or interesting history behind them. Each card becomes a chapter in the story of their travels.

In this way, your display becomes more than just a way to store your items—it transforms into a visual narrative that captivates both you and anyone who sees it.

4.4 Protecting Your Collection: Ensuring Longevity

Whatever collectibles you decide to collect, it will definitely involve delicate items, and often times those are the most rarest and the most valuable. Different items in your collection will require different care depending on the materials they're made of. Paper-based items, like vintage posters or rare books, need to be stored in acid-free packaging to prevent yellowing. Meanwhile, wooden items should be kept out of humid areas to avoid warping, and metal objects need to be protected from rust.

A good friend of mine collects antique maps from different era. He learned the hard way that storing them in regular plastic sleeves led to discoloration. After consulting a preservation expert, he switched to archival-quality materials, and now, each map is stored in a climate-controlled room with UV-protective glass. Now, the maps are safe and intact as well as they are displayed attractively for visitors like us.

Environmental factors like temperature and humidity can damage delicate items. If you decide collect vintage comic books or antique artworks, keeping these in a room that fluctuates wildly between hot and cold, or becomes too humid, can cause pages to wrinkle, ink to fade, or frames to crack, which will heavily damage the collectibles and decrease their value greatly.

A stamp collector must have a special cabinet with climate control specifically designed to keep his collection in pristine condition. While this might sound extreme, even simple adjustments—like using a dehumidifier or storing valuable items in a cool, dark space—can help protect them from damage over time and ensure their preservation.

Handling valuable or delicate items can be nerve-wrecking. If you're dealing with particularly fragile objects, such as porcelain or rare photographs, taking precautions like wearing gloves can make a world of difference.

When I inherited my late grandmother's vintage jewelry collection, I learned from a jeweler how to properly clean and store each piece. Using soft cloths, non-abrasive cleaning solutions, and storing them in velvet-lined boxes has kept the collection in immaculate condition, preserving both its sentimental and material value.

4.5 Displaying Without Damaging: Protection Meets Presentation

Proper Mounting Techniques: Safe and Stylish Display

Mounting and framing are essential to displaying certain types of collections. Whether it's photographs, artwork, or memorabilia, knowing how to mount these items properly can prevent irreversible damage. Archival-quality frames and UV-protective glass are ideal for preserving photos and prints.

A collector of sports memorabilia I met used frameless glass cases for his autographed baseballs collection. The cases allowed the items to be admired from all angles while protecting them from dust and direct contact.

Avoiding Sunlight and Dust Exposure

Sunlight is one of the biggest enemies of a collection. The UV rays can cause colors to fade, paper to yellow, and fabric to deteriorate. Dust, too, can build up and slowly wear down the surface of items.

If you're displaying your collection in a sunny room, consider using UV-filtering glass or simply rotating items in and out of display to limit exposure. A vinyl record collector I know keeps a portion of his collection in open shelving, but rotates which albums are on display to prevent any long-term exposure to dust and sunlight.

4.6 Organizing for Future Expansion of Your Collection: Thinking Ahead

If you are dedicated enough, your collection is destined to grow over time, often in unexpected and unusual ways. Whether you're actively adding to it or receiving new items as gifts, it's always important to leave room for growth when organizing your collection, so you don't get into chaos when you receive your new collectibles.

A collector who collects comic books must have modular shelves that can be adjusted as his collection grows. He needs to keep extra space on each shelf for future additions, which would make integrating new comics seamless and prevents overcrowding. Planning for growth now ensures that your collection remains functional and organized as it evolves.

One way to manage a growing collection is to rotate your displays. You don't have to showcase everything at once. Regularly swapping out items keeps your space feeling fresh and gives each piece its moment to shine. It might sound like a tiresome task, but if you are really into your collection then this would be the activity you would wait around for cause it gives you the chance to connect with your collection from time to time.

For example, an art collector I know rotates her collection every few months. She has more pieces than she can display at once, so she selects a new theme for each season. This not only keeps her home looking different but also allows her to focus on appreciating individual pieces more deeply.

4.7 Balancing Storage and Display: Maximizing Space and Enjoyment

Deciding what to display and what to store can be tricky. Some items may be too valuable or fragile to leave out in the open, while others are perfect for daily enjoyment.

A collector of vintage toy cars once told me that he displays his everyday favorites but keeps the rarest models in specially designed storage boxes. This way, he can enjoy the bulk of his collection while ensuring that the most delicate and valuable pieces are well-protected.

Even if something isn't currently on display, it should still be stored or packaged safely. Labeling boxes clearly and storing items in proper conditions (such as acid-free materials for paper items) ensures that they're ready for future display or use without having deteriorated in storage.

4.8 Sharing Your Collection: Building Connections Through Your Passion

Sharing your collection with others can be an incredibly rewarding experience, turning what might be a solitary hobby into an opportunity for connection and inspiration. Imagine inviting a few friends over for a casual gathering, not just to admire your collection but to share the stories behind each piece. Whether it's vintage cameras, rare comic books, retro video games or antique glassware, your collection is an extension of you and your personality—and sharing it can spark fascinating conversations and experience.

A good example of this is the friend of mine, mentioned before, who collects antique cameras. Rather than keeping them hidden away, he often hosts small "photography appreciation nights" where fellow enthusiasts can come over and handle the cameras, swap tips, and discuss their latest finds. His home transforms into a mini-gallery, and each event strengthens the connections he's made within the community. Not only does he share his passion, but he also learns from others in ways that deepen his appreciation for the collection.

For those who prefer the digital world, sharing your collection online can open up even more doors. A friend of mine, another vintage camera enthusiast, started a blog where he not only showcases his collection but also writes about the history behind each camera and its significance. Over time, his blog attracted a community of readers and fellow collectors who began sharing their own insights and experiences in the comments. What started as a personal project turned into a platform for connection and learning.

Social media is another great avenue. Platforms like Instagram or Pinterest allow you to share curated images of your collection with a global audience. Whether it's close-up shots of rare stamps or a photo series of your favorite art pieces, these platforms help connect you with others who share your passion, often leading to friendships or even new acquisitions!

Another meaningful way to share your collection is through documentation. Taking the time to photograph or record your collection creates a lasting archive, allowing you to preserve its legacy and share it with future generations. This practice not only captures the beauty of your items but also tells the story behind each one—how you acquired it, why it's special, and the journey it represents.

Take, for example, a woman I know who has been collecting rare books for decades. As her collection grew, she realized that each book carried its own unique history—whether it was a first edition of a beloved novel or a beautifully bound poetry collection passed down from her grandmother. She began photographing each book, carefully documenting where and when she acquired it, as well as the personal memories attached. What started as a simple record evolved into a digital archive, complete with stories that her children and grandchildren could one day enjoy. This project not only preserves the value of her collection but also keeps alive the emotional connection she has with each piece.

This process of documentation is especially important for collectors of fragile or perishable items. A photographer I once met, who specializes in collecting vintage postcards, has started scanning and archiving his collection. Over time, the delicate paper and ink will inevitably fade, but with his digital archive, the postcards' images and stories will live on for future generations to enjoy. This way, he's not only preserving the physical collection but also creating a legacy that can be shared long after the original items have aged.

4.9 Enjoying Your Collection Every Day

A collection is not meant to be locked away or admired only on special occasions—it's something that should bring you joy and happiness every day when you go through them. One of the most rewarding aspects of collecting is finding ways to integrate your cherished items into your daily routine, transforming your living space into a reflection of your passions.

Consider the example of a collector I know who has a deep love for vintage watches. Rather than storing them in a drawer or keeping them tucked away in a display case, he wears a different watch every day. It's not about showing off—it's about experiencing the craftsmanship and history behind each piece in a tangible way and enjoying the company of the collectibles that he hustled so hard to acquire. By rotating through his collection, he brings new life to each watch, appreciating them not just as objects but as companions in his daily life.

Similarly, a friend of mine collects antique clocks. While many might see these as purely decorative, he has made them an integral part of his home. A few of his favorite pieces are prominently displayed in the living room, and the steady ticking of the clocks creates a calming ambiance that fills the space. These clocks don't just sit there; they become part of the rhythm of his home, a quiet reminder of his passion for craftsmanship and history.

Whether it's showcasing your rare books on a beautiful bookshelf, using vintage china for special dinners, or hanging your favorite prints in a prominent space at your house, your collection deserves to be part of your everyday environment. By doing this, you create an intimate connection with the items you've spent so much time acquiring, making each piece a small, daily source of joy.

At the heart of every collection lies the joy of reflection. As you curate, organize, and display your collection, it's important to step back and appreciate the journey that brought you here. Each item represents more than just an object—it holds memories, emotions, and the story of your evolving interests.

For many collectors, reflection is the most rewarding aspect of the process. A friend of mine, who collects vintage concert posters, shared how he often sits with his collection and remembers the concerts he attended, the friends he made, and the experiences that shaped his life. It's not just about the posters themselves; it's about reliving those moments and cherishing how they've become a part of who he is today.

Another collector I know, who focuses on antique pottery, says that whenever she feels stressed, she takes a few minutes to admire her collection. The colors, textures, and craftsmanship remind her of the joy she felt when she first discovered each piece. In those moments, she feels a deep sense of contentment, knowing that her collection reflects her personality, her history, and her passions.

Your collection is a reflection of you. It represents the hours you've spent researching, the moments of excitement when you found a rare piece, and the pride you feel in seeing it all come together. As you continue to grow and nurture your collection, remember to take time to reflect on how far you've come. Each item is a testament to your curiosity, dedication, and love for the art of collecting.

So, take a deep breath, step back, and let your collection remind you of the joy it brings to your life every single day.

By taking thoughtful steps to protect and showcase your items, you not only preserve their value but also enhance your own enjoyment of them. Your collection, after all, is a reflection of your passions—so treat it with the care and love it deserves.

Chapter 5: Understanding the Value of
Your Collection

As I have stating continuously stating, collecting isn't just about accumulating things—it's about finding pieces that resonate with the passion within you, understanding their significance, and recognizing their proper worth. This chapter will be your guide to understanding the multi-dimensional value of your collections, from emotional to financial, and learning how to protect and even pass it down to future generations.

5.1 Learn about The Different Types of Value

Sentimental Value

Sometimes, the true value of a collection can't be measured in dollars and cents. Imagine your grandmother's hundred years old tea set, the one passed down through generations. While it may not fetch much at an auction, its value to you and your family is immeasurable because it carries memories of family's history and generational gatherings and warm cups of tea shared on holiday afternoons. This is what we call **sentimental value**—the emotional connection you have to an item, which often outweighs its market price!

Family heirlooms, childhood toys, or objects tied to significant life events can become priceless in your eyes. Think of a worn-out baseball glove that's been with you since you were a kid—no collector would pay top dollar for it, but to you, it's irreplaceable because it tells a story. Your collection might be full of these emotional touchstones, items that bring you joy simply because they remind you of a time, a place, or a person!

Financial Value

On the other side of the coin (sometimes quite literally), there's **financial value**. Certain collectibles, like rare coins, retro action figures, or first-edition books, can significantly increase in worth with time. Take vintage comic books, for instance—what was once a casual pastime for many has now turned into a multi-million-dollar market. A pristine copy of *Action Comics #1*, which originally sold for 10 cents in 1938, was auctioned for over $3 million.

But how do you determine if something has financial value? It often comes down to factors like rarity, condition, and demand. A rare *Star Wars* action figure in mint condition can be worth thousands, while a common figure with wear and tear might only be worth a few dollars. Knowing how to spot these differences is key to understanding the financial dimension of your collection.

Cultural and Historical Significance

Then there's cultural and historical value—items that capture and points to a moment in time or reflect a significant cultural or historical movement. Think of memorabilia from World War II or the first moon landing. These objects don't just have financial worth; they represent key moments in history. Owning a piece of that history makes the item more than just a collectible; it becomes a unbreakable connection to a shared past.

Cultural items, such as an original *Star Wars* poster or a guitar signed by a legendary rock band, have a similar appeal. They capture the essence of an era, and their value is often tied to the lasting impact of the event or cultural movement they represent. These items are often high in value, not just because they're rare, but because they are symbols of a time that still echoes with people today.

5.2 How to Appraise Your Collection

For those new to collecting, the first step in understanding the value of your items is through **self-appraisal**. While it may not give you a perfectly accurate figure, doing your own research can help set realistic and grounded expectations. Start by looking at auction results, checking **collector price guides**, and browsing online marketplaces like eBay. Pay attention to recent sales, not just asking prices, to get a true sense of the market.

For example, if you're trying to determine the worth of a vintage vinyl record, compare your copy to others that have recently sold in auctions or online listings. Is your record in similar condition? Does it have the original sleeve or insert or scratches on the record? These details and comparisons can significantly affect the value, and while self-appraisal isn't foolproof, it's a great way to get a ballpark figure.

Then, if you suspect an item in your collection is particularly rare or valuable, it might be time to consider getting a **professional appraisal**. Professional appraisers specialize in evaluating collectibles and can provide a detailed and accurate value, often necessary for high-value collectibles, insurance purposes, or before selling or pawning the item. For instance, if you have a signed first-edition novel, it's worth the investment to get a professional opinion on its worth based on the publication, author or the novel's history or influence on the culture.

Finding the right appraiser can be as simple as reaching out to antique dealers, contacting certified specialists, or looking within niche communities like sports memorabilia or vintage furniture. You might be surprised to know that, you can find appraisers for all sorts of collectibles, from movie memorabilia to vintage toys to ancients pottery. So, don't think your collection is odd or strange, rather it might be the one that is the most valuable in your showcase.

Factors Appraisers Consider

Appraisers use several criteria to determine an item's value, including the following primary factors:

- **Age**: Generally, the older an item, the more valuable it may be, though this isn't always the case.
- **Condition**: An item in mint or near-mint condition is always worth more. A rare comic book with a crease or torn page will fetch less than a flawless one.
- **Provenance**: This refers to the item's history. If you have a baseball signed by Babe Ruth with documentation proving its authenticity, sky's the limit for the price of that piece!
- **Rarity and Demand**: An item might be rare, but if there's little demand for it in the current market, its value won't be as high. Conversely, a common item that's in high demand at the time can see prices skyrocket!

5.3 Protecting Your Collection with Insurance

If your collection holds significant financial or sentimental value, insuring it is crucial. Imagine the heartbreak of losing a prized valuable collection to theft, fire, or accidental damage. Insurance lets you have peace of mind, ensuring that in case of an unfortunate event, you won't lose everything. Whether it's a collection of rare coins or valuable sports memorabilia, insurance can cover both replacement costs and potential appreciation over time.

Not all insurance policies are created equal. While your **homeowner's policy** might provide some coverage for your collectibles, it often falls short for higher-value items or specific types of collections. That's where **specialized insurance policies** come in, offering better coverage, including protection against depreciation and even for items on loan or display. When choosing a policy, ensure it covers the full value of your collection and any risks specific to how you store or display it. For example, a typical homeowner's insurance policy may limit coverage to $2,500 for collectibles, which is often insufficient for valuable items like vintage watches, rare art, or comic book collections.

This is where **specialized insurance** comes in. These policies are designed to offer more comprehensive protection for high-value collections, including coverage for depreciation, damage, theft, and even items on loan or display outside your home. Here are a few companies that specialize in collectible insurance:

- **Collectibles Insurance Services**: One of the most well-known providers, they offer policies tailored for a wide range of collectibles, including comic books, sports memorabilia, stamps, coins, and more. Their coverage is flexible, protecting against risks like accidental damage, natural disasters, and theft.
- **AXA Art**: AXA specializes in fine art and collectibles insurance, covering everything from artwork to rare antiques. They offer coverage for collectors, galleries, and museums, and their policies extend to items in transit or on display at exhibitions.
- **American Collectors Insurance**: This company focuses on insuring vintage and classic cars but also offers coverage for other collectibles like firearms, antiques, and model trains. Their policies include options for agreed value coverage, meaning they'll pay the full insured value in the event of a loss, without depreciation.
- **Chubb**: Chubb is a global insurer that provides high-value coverage for personal property, including art, jewelry, and collectibles. They offer tailored policies that can cover entire collections, providing protection against theft, damage, and even restoration costs.

Note that these are some examples from my side, you have to do your own research while choosing the insurance that suits you best. When choosing a policy, ensure it covers the full value of your collection and any risks specific to how you store or display your items. For instance, if you frequently loan pieces to museums or display them at conventions, make sure your policy covers these situations. Look for coverage that includes accidental damage, loss in transit, and protection against depreciation, ensuring your collection is fully protected.

To secure proper insurance, documenting your collection is key. Keep a detailed inventory that includes item descriptions, purchase dates, and appraisals. High-quality photos can serve as proof of condition, while receipts or certificates of authenticity further validate the value of your items. Store these documents safely—both in physical form and digitally—so they're easily accessible if needed.

5.4 Factors That Affect Market Value

Rarity and Scarcity

An item's rarity often plays the biggest role in its value. The fewer items there are, the more collectors are willing to pay. This is especially true for collectibles that are hard to find or no longer made. Rarity isn't just about how many were made, but how many remain in good condition. If only a handful of items survive in pristine condition, their value skyrockets. For example:

- **Limited-edition action figures**: A rare *Star Wars* action figure, like the 1978 "Rocket-Firing Boba Fett," was never released to the public due to safety concerns. Only a few prototypes exist, and one was sold at auction for over $150,000!

- **Discontinued luxury watches**: The **Rolex Daytona "Paul Newman"** is a highly sought-after vintage watch. Originally not popular, it became incredibly rare when production stopped. In 2017, Paul Newman's personal Daytona sold for a staggering $17.8 million, setting a record for wristwatch sales.
- **Rare comic books**: A copy of *Action Comics #1*, which introduced Superman in 1938, is one of the most famous rare comics. In mint condition, one of these comics was sold for over $3 million in 2014!

Rarity isn't just about how many were made, but also how many remain in good condition. If only a few items survive in near-perfect shape, their value skyrockets. For instance, a **first-edition Harry Potter book** (1997) in pristine condition was sold for $471,000 in 2021 because most copies were heavily used or damaged over the years.

As items become harder to find, and if they remain in excellent condition, their prices often soar, making them incredibly valuable to collectors.

Condition and Preservation

Even the rarest collectible can lose a lot of its value if it's not well taken care of. The overall condition of an item plays a huge role in determining how much it's worth. For example, a first-edition book from a famous author, like *The Great Gatsby* by F. Scott Fitzgerald, could be worth tens of thousands of dollars in mint condition. However, if the cover is torn, the pages are stained, or the spine is damaged, its value could drop dramatically. A damaged first-edition might only sell for a fraction of what a pristine copy would!

Another example is vintage baseball cards. A **1952 Mickey Mantle rookie card** in perfect condition once sold for $12.6 million, making it the most expensive sports card ever. However, if the same card is bent, has creases, or shows signs of wear, it might only sell for a few thousand dollars or even less!

As a collector, taking care of your items is key to maintaining or even increasing their value. Proper storage—such as keeping items in protective cases, away from sunlight, moisture, and dust—can help preserve their condition. For example, keeping a vinyl record collection stored upright, in a cool, dry place, and handling them carefully to avoid scratches can help retain or boost their value over time. In contrast, a scratched or warped record is far less valuable than one kept in perfect condition.

By maintaining your collectibles and repairing minor damages when needed, you can keep their value intact and potentially see them increase over time!

Provenance and History

Provenance, or the history behind an item, adds a special story that can make it far more valuable. It's not just about owning something rare—knowing where it came from and being able to prove its background makes a huge difference in the price collectors are willing to pay.

For example, **a baseball signed by Babe Ruth** is highly valuable on its own, but if it comes with documentation proving it was signed at the 1932 World Series, when Ruth famously called his shot, the value will increase thousandfold. A ball like this could sell for hundreds of thousands of dollars, while a similar signed baseball without clear history might go for far less than that.

Another example is artwork. A painting by a famous artist like **Claude Monet** is already worth millions, but if it comes with records showing it was part of a prominent art collection, such as being owned by a royal family or displayed in a major museum, its value might increase dramatically. Having this verified history, or provenance, reassures buyers that the piece is authentic and significant, which pushes the price higher.

Even vintage guitars have higher value with strong provenance. For instance, a guitar used by **Jimi Hendrix** in a concert is worth much more if there is proof of its use, like photographs or concert records. Without this history, the guitar is still valuable, but collectors are willing to pay much more for an instrument tied to a legendary performance!

The more detailed and trustworthy the history behind an item, the higher its value becomes! Proper documentation, such as certificates of authenticity, auction records, or historical photos, can make all the difference in what collectors are willing to pay.

Trends and Timing

The market for collectibles can be just as unpredictable as the stock market. What's popular and valuable today might lose its shine tomorrow, while something forgotten could suddenly become highly sought after. Trends in the collectibles world often rise and fall due to pop culture events, anniversaries, or renewed interest in certain themes.

For example, when Marvel movies became a massive hit, the demand for original comic books featuring characters like Iron Man and Spider-Man soared. A **1962 Amazing Fantasy #15**, the first appearance of Spider-Man, sold for over $3 million in 2021. However, years ago, before the Marvel movies became a global phenomenon, the same comic might have sold for much less!

Another good example is vintage Pokémon cards. When Pokémon had its 20th anniversary, there was a surge in interest, especially for the original cards from the 1990s. A **1999 first-edition Charizard card** that used to be worth a few hundred dollars can now sell for over $300,000 if it's in mint condition! The timing of the anniversary, along with the resurgence of Pokémon's popularity, caused the market for these cards to spike.

Even vintage movie posters see their value rise and fall based on timing. For instance, the release of new **Star Wars** films in recent years drove up demand for memorabilia from the original 1977 movie. Posters, action figures, and other items from that era became much more valuable because of the renewed interest and popularity among the new generation in the franchise.

To maximize the value of your collection, it's important to stay informed about trends and time your sales wisely. Something that's in demand now may lose value in a few years, while holding onto certain items until a key anniversary or pop culture moment might help you cash in at the right time...

5.5 When and How to Sell

Timing is everything when it comes to selling a collection. Waiting for the right moment, such as when demand peaks or after an item has appreciated in value, can result in higher valuation. But hold on too long, and the market could shift! Knowing when to sell is about understanding the trends and your own visions.

Different items sell better in different platforms. Online auction sites like eBay offer a wide audience but may come with hefty fees. Local antique shops might give you a quick sale but at a lower price and also they might not have the proper valuation for the piece. For high-value or rare items, specialized auctions like Heritage Auctions may be the best route. Consider the pros and cons of each before listing your items for sale.

When it comes to negotiating, understanding the true value of your items is key. Don't be afraid to counter offers or walk away from a deal if it doesn't feel right... Whether in person or online, approach negotiations with confidence and proper knowledge of your item's worth.

5.6 Understanding Long-Term Investment Potential

While collecting can indeed be considered a financial investment, not all items will appreciate in value. The key is to focus on quality over quantity—purchasing rare, well-preserved items with cultural or historical significance. However, the market can be volatile, so it's essential to be aware of the risks involved.

Certain collectibles have proven to be solid investments. For example, vintage comic books and first-edition novels have consistently risen in value as their rarity and cultural impact increases day by day. Items that were once considered ordinary and worthless have become prized treasures over the decades, turning hobbies into profitable ventures.

Now, it's easy to get caught up in the lucrative idea of making money from your collection, but remember— passion should always come first. Always keep in mind why you started collecting in the first place. The most successful collectors often follow their hearts, and the financial rewards come naturally over time. By collecting what you love, you ensure that even if the market dips, your collection will still hold immense value to you.

5.7 Passing Down Your Collection

Your collection is more than just a group of items—it's a time capsule filled with stories, memories, and meaning. When passed down, it can become a cherished family heirloom, carrying both sentimental and financial value. Whether it's a carefully curated set of vintage baseball cards, a collection of antique jewelry, or even rare vinyl records, these items can connect future generations to their history in a deeply personal way.

For example, consider a collection of vintage baseball cards that spans decades of the sport's history. The 1952 Mickey Mantle card may be worth millions today, but beyond the dollar signs, it's also a window into the golden era of baseball, representing the passion and dedication of the collector who spent years building it. Imagine handing that history down to your grandchildren—something they can treasure not just for its worth but for the stories it carries about their family's past.

To ensure your collection stands the test of time, thorough documentation is key. This includes keeping records of each item's provenance, condition, and value, as well as any stories or memories attached to them. After all, a collection's true worth isn't just in its market value—it's in the love and care you've poured into it.

Selling vs. Inheriting: A Personal Choice

Deciding whether to sell your collection or pass it down is one of the most personal decisions a collector can make. Some collectors choose to sell their items while they're still alive, enjoying the financial rewards of a well-maintained collection. For example, the owner of a rare Action Comics #1 might decide to sell it for millions to fund their retirement or to fulfill other financial goals.

On the other hand, many collectors find comfort in leaving their collection as a legacy for loved ones, allowing the stories and significance behind the items to live on. Think of a vintage coin collection passed down through generations—each coin may carry its own unique story, and preserving these tales ensures that future generations don't just inherit objects, but a piece of their family's identity.

Interestingly, some collections have gone on to increase in value dramatically after being inherited. The art collection of Peggy and David Rockefeller, for instance, became one of the largest estate auctions in history, fetching over $835 million after their passing. The Rockefeller family, known for their deep love of art, passed down more than wealth—they passed down an enduring legacy of culture and appreciation.

Whether you choose to sell or pass down your collection, remember that both paths have their own rewards. Selling allows you to enjoy the fruits of your hard work during your lifetime, while passing it down ensures your collection's stories continue to inspire and connect future generations. Either way, your collection's impact will extend far beyond the items themselves.

I guess now we've explored the many dimensions of value that come with collecting, from personal sentiment to market trends. Whether you're just starting or you're looking to sell, understanding the true worth of your collection—emotionally, financially, and historically—is key to making informed decisions and ensuring your treasures continue to bring joy, both now and in the future.

Chapter 6: Navigating the World of Online Collecting

The internet has fundamentally transformed countless aspects of life, and for collectors, it has been nothing short of a revolution. Where a collector once had to rely on local shops, flea markets, or the occasional trade show, garage sales, the digital age has unleashed a global marketplace, opening up the door to new possibilities that collectors from earlier generations could only dream of. Let's dive into the opportunities and challenges of collecting in an online world—from finding rare items across the globe to building a community with fellow collectors, to avoiding the dangers of scams and counterfeits. We'll explore how you can make the most of online platforms, auctions, and social media to maximize the fun in your collecting journey.

6.1 The Rise of Online Collecting

Imagine a time when collecting meant rummaging through dusty old shops, attending local fairs, or keeping an eye out at neighborhood garage sales. These treasure hunts had their charm, but they were often limited by your location and what events you could attend. If you were hunting for a rare coin or vintage book, your best chance might have been a once-a-year local fair or hoping you got lucky at a yard sale or your financial position to travel abroad.

Today, the internet has completely changed that process. Collecting is no longer limited by location or timing. With just a few clicks, you can explore rare and unique items from anywhere in the world without leaving your home. Whether you're looking for a specific comic book, a piece of antique furniture, or a rare vinyl record, the digital world has put global markets right at your fingertips.

Platforms like eBay, Etsy, and even social media have connected collectors and sellers across continents. For example, if you're searching for a rare Pokémon card from the 1990s, you can now find a seller in Japan or Canada offering exactly what you need. Or perhaps you're a fan of vintage typewriters—what used to take years of searching can now be found in minutes by browsing through listings from across the globe.

Think of it like upgrading from a small neighborhood flea market to a massive international bazaar. In the past, a collector of antique postcards might spend hours driving to different towns or even flying to another country, hoping to find something new. Now, that same collector can browse listings from Tokyo, Toronto, or Berlin—all in a single evening.

This global access has redefined how collectors can approach their hobby nowadays. The possibilities feel almost endless, and the convenience of searching, buying, and trading from the comfort of your couch has opened up a whole new world of collecting.

Before the internet, finding a rare collectible meant hoping to stumble across it locally or spending months—if not years—tracking it down through personal networks. Now, thanks to global online marketplaces, you can source collectibles from countries you may never visit in person. A vintage toy collector in New York might score a rare item from a seller in Japan, or a book lover in France could complete their collection with a first edition sourced from an independent dealer in Australia. The world is truly at your fingertips.

This global access also means that competition for rare items can be fiercer than ever. While you're hunting for that one-of-a-kind item, collectors on the other side of the globe are doing the same, often leading to bidding wars or rising prices. The key is to know where to look and how to make informed purchases, which we'll explore in the next section.

6.2 Finding and Buying Collectibles Online

Navigating the world of online collecting begins with knowing where to look. A few platforms that dominate the scene are:

- **eBay**: A giant in the online marketplace world, eBay remains the go-to for many collectors. It offers a wide range of categories, from vintage toys to rare coins, and allows for both auction-style bidding and direct sales. While it's user-friendly, fees can be high, and you'll need to watch out for competitive bidding.
- **Etsy**: Known for its artisan goods and handmade items, Etsy is also a haven for vintage lovers. It's especially good for niche items and smaller collectibles, such as vintage jewelry or antique home décor. The platform is highly user-friendly but has fewer high-end collectibles.
- **Heritage Auctions and Bonhams**: For more serious collectors, these auction houses are perfect for high-value items like rare artwork, coins, or luxury timepieces. However, they can come with steep fees and require a more in-depth understanding of the auction process.

Each platform offers different advantages, so it's essential to choose based on your needs, whether it's accessibility, variety, or the ability to bid in real-time.

You might think that due to the dramatic rise of online collection platforms, the thrill of the hunt is still alive! If you know how to look… Scoring a great deal or discovering a hidden gem is like unearthing a diamond in the rough. To do this, patience is crucial. Instead of simply browsing, use **strategic search terms**. For example, rather than typing "vintage clock," search for a specific brand, model, or year to narrow down your results.

Another tip: set up **alerts or notifications** for new listings on these platforms. Many platforms offer this feature, so you can be one of the first to know when a coveted item becomes available. Expanding your search across multiple platforms increases your chances of success. Some platforms even have **email**

lists that provide valuable insights into vintage, retro collectible products as well as current market trends and future predictions. Finally, persistence does pays off—checking listings regularly will help you catch deals that others may neglect!

Before making any purchase, it's vital to evaluate both the seller and the listing carefully. Always start by reading reviews and checking feedback ratings. A seller with consistently high ratings is usually a safer bet than someone with mixed or no reviews.

Be alert of listings with vague descriptions or low-quality photos. If a seller doesn't provide clear, detailed information about an item, it might be a red flag! When in doubt, ask for additional photos or documentation to confirm authenticity. If a seller is hesitant to offer more information, trust your gut—it might be better to walk away.

6.3 Buying Safely: Avoiding Scams and Counterfeits

The world of online collecting can be a treasure trove of exciting finds, but it can also be a minefield filled with scams! Unfortunately, the more popular online collecting has become, the more scams have emerged. It's important to know what to look for so you don't fall victim to some of the most common traps.

Common Online Scams

One of the most frequent scams is the **fake listing**. This happens when a seller posts an item, like a rare action figure or an autographed baseball, but the item doesn't actually exist. You might pay, expecting your prized collectible to arrive, only to realize the seller has vanished into thin air. Imagine thinking you've just bought a rare vintage Star Wars figure from the 1980s, only to never hear from the seller again, and your money is gone.

Another common scam involves **counterfeit items**. For instance, a collector might think they're buying a first-edition comic book, but when it arrives, it's a cleverly produced fake. Some scammers are very skilled, so you need to be careful and experienced. If the price seems too good to be true, that's often a red flag!!

To protect yourself, always check the seller's **feedback and history** on the platform. If they have poor reviews, or if they've just joined and haven't sold much, it might be a sign they aren't trustworthy. Remember, if a deal feels too good to be true, it probably is.

How to Verify Authenticity

When it comes to valuable collectibles, **authenticity is everything**. Here's how you can make sure you're getting the real deal:

- **Request certificates of authenticity** (COAs) for high-value items. For example, if you're buying a signed sports jersey, ask for a COA from a trusted source.
- Ask for **extra real-time photos** that show unique details of the item, like serial numbers or special markings. A seller with nothing to hide will be happy to provide more images.
- Use **online communities or forums** to ask experienced collectors for advice. These groups can help you spot a fake or avoid a shady seller. For instance, if you're buying a rare coin, coin collector forums are full of experts who can help you verify its authenticity.

In the end, **trust your instincts.** If something feels off—whether it's the price, the seller's behavior, or the lack of information—don't rush into the purchase.

Using Secure Payment Methods

When making online purchases, always use secure payment methods. PayPal and credit cards are great options because they offer buyer protection. This means if something goes wrong—like the item doesn't arrive or isn't what was promised—you can get your money back. Avoid wire transfers or non-secure payment options because once you send the money, it's gone, and you have no recourse.

For example, a collector buying a vintage video game might pay through PayPal. If the seller disappears or the game arrives damaged, they can file a dispute and potentially get a refund. It's worth sticking to platforms that offer these kinds of protections—it's a small step that can save you a lot of pain and hassles later!

6.4 Leveraging Social Media for Collecting

Social media has turned into a goldmine for collectors looking to connect with others who share their passion. Platforms like **Facebook**, **Instagram**, **Reddit**, and **X (previously Twitter)** aren't just for sharing photos of your lunch or trips—they're also amazing tools for connecting with other collectors or enthusiasts from around the world. Many collectors use these platforms to share their latest finds, give advice on how to spot rare items, and participate in groups that are focused on very specific types of collectibles.

For instance, you could join a Facebook group dedicated to vintage action figures, where members share tips on finding hidden gems or help authenticate items. X (previously Twitter), on the other hand, is great for following industry trends and connecting with experts in your field. It's like having access to a global community of people who get just as excited about collectibles as you do. Reddit also has great and large communities related to specific niches where you can connect with like-minded enthusiasts and collectors.

One of the biggest benefits of social media is the ability to join specialized online collector communities. These groups, such as **Facebook groups**, **Reddit forums**, or niche websites, allow collectors to network with others who share their specific interests. Whether you're into rare coins, vintage watches, or antique books, there's probably a community out there for you.

These online spaces are often a treasure trove of insider knowledge. You'll find experienced collectors sharing advice on how to care for certain items, exclusive listings for rare pieces, or even offers to trade or sell within the community. It's a fantastic way to broaden your horizons and learn from others who have been in the game for years!

Visual platforms like **Instagram** and **YouTube** are perfect for showing off your collection to the world. Not only can you document your journey as a collector, but you can also connect with a wider audience. On Instagram, for example, you can post high-quality photos of your items, use hashtags to reach lots of others in your niche, and engage with followers who share your enthusiasm.

YouTube takes it a step further! By creating videos that showcase your collection or your journey towards getting to new collectibles, you can offer detailed insights into your pieces, tell the story behind each find, and even do unboxing videos for newly acquired items. These platforms can help you attract potential buyers or even sellers with unusual rare items, build a community around your hobby, and even earn recognition as an expert in your field.

6.5 Bidding in Online Auctions

Online auctions are one of the most exciting ways to buy collectibles. Platforms like **eBay** and specialized auction houses like **Christie's** or **Sotheby's** allow collectors to bid on rare and valuable items from anywhere in the world. Here's how it works: a seller lists an item, sets a starting price, and collectors can place their bids over a set period. The highest bidder at the end of the auction wins the item.

Navigating these platforms can be tricky, especially if you're new to online auctions. Each site has its own quirks—eBay is known for its mix of everyday items and rarities, while Christie's focuses on high-end auctions. Understanding how the platform works is the first step to becoming a savvy bidder.

Before you dive headfirst into bidding, it's important to set a definite budget. Auctions can get heated, and it's easy to get caught up in the excitement and bid more than you intend to. Decide on a maximum price you're willing to pay for an item and stick to it, no matter how tempting it is to keep bidding! And if it get too out of hands, it's better for you to let it go, and wait for the next big thing. No shame in it!

There are also different bidding strategies to consider. Some collectors prefer to place bids early, hoping to scare off competition. Others use the **sniping strategy**, where they wait until the last minute to place a bid, giving other bidders less time to react. Whichever approach you choose, staying calm and sticking to your budget is the key.

Winning Auctions Without Breaking the Bank

Winning an auction without overspending requires a bit of strategy and planning. One tip is to target auctions that takes place during less competitive timeframes, such as late at night or on weekdays, when fewer people are bidding. You can also look for items that haven't started trending yet—this way, you can snag them before the prices skyrocket.

Avoid getting caught up in bidding wars, where two or more bidders drive up the price far beyond the item's actual value. It can be tempting to outbid someone just for the adrenaline rush for the win, but it's important to know when to walk away!

6.6 Selling Your Collection Online

If you're looking to sell part or all of your collection, choosing the right platform is significant. Sites like **eBay, Etsy,** and **Facebook Marketplace** etc. each offer different advantages. For instance, eBay is great for items of all values, while Etsy is better suited for vintage or handmade goods. If you have high-value items, auction houses like **Heritage Auctions** or **Bonhams** might be a better fit, though they tend to come with higher fees!

It's important to consider both the audience and the fees involved with each platform. For everyday collectibles, eBay or Facebook Marketplace might be the easiest and most cost-effective option. For rarer, more valuable pieces, auction houses can attract serious and genuine buyers willing to pay a premium and appreciate the value of your collectible.

Creating Effective Listings

The secret to selling collectibles online is creating effective listings. Start by writing detailed descriptions that provide all the information a potential buyer would need to get interested—this includes the item's condition, any wear and tear, its origin, and, if applicable, its authenticity.

High-quality photos are also compulsory. Make sure to capture the item from multiple angles, and highlight any unique features. The more transparent and detailed you are, the more likely you'll attract serious and original buyers.

Setting Fair Prices

Setting a fair price can be a challenge, but it's vital to get it right! Research similar items that have recently sold on the platform to get a sense of the going rate. It's also important to factor in any fees the platform might charge, as well as the current demand and trends for the item. Pricing too high might scare away genuine buyers, while pricing too low could mean leaving money on the table and undervaluing your precious collection.

6.7 Building an Online Presence as a Collector

Building an online presence as a collector can dramatically enhance your reputation, increase your sales, and connect you with a wider community. Whether you're buying, selling, or simply showcasing your prized items, a strong and trustworthy online persona helps set you apart from the crowd. Here are more tips and strategies to help you become a recognized figure in the world of collecting.

Becoming a Recognized Seller or Collector

If you want to be known as a respected collector or seller, your online reputation is everything. Whether you're selling on eBay, Etsy, or other platforms, it's important to be seen as trustworthy, reliable, and knowledgeable. Here are several ways to build that recognition:

- **Deliver consistent service**: Always communicate promptly and professionally with buyers or fellow collectors. Pack your items securely, ship them on time, and always describe your items accurately. Going the extra mile to make sure your buyers have a smooth experience can lead to positive reviews and repeat customers.
- **Earn positive feedback**: Reviews matter. Encourage satisfied buyers to leave feedback, and respond politely to any negative reviews. If there's an issue, try to resolve it quickly and fairly. A good track record of handling problems professionally can build trust.
- **Be active in your niche**: Join forums, Facebook groups, or Reddit threads related to your area of expertise. Answer questions, offer advice, and participate in discussions. The more visible and helpful you are, the more you'll be recognized as an expert.
- **Offer transparency**: Always be transparent about the condition and authenticity of the items you sell. Posting clear, high-quality photos from multiple angles, along with detailed descriptions, shows that you're honest and knowledgeable. Buyers will trust you more when they know exactly what they're getting.
- **Showcase your passion**: Passion is contagious. When people see how much you care about your collection, whether through your posts or listings, they'll be more likely to engage with you. For example, sharing the backstory behind a rare item you've found or your journey as a collector can add a personal touch that builds loyalty.

Networking with Influencers and Collectors

To grow your presence even further, networking with other well-known collectors or influencers in your niche is key. This can lead to collaborations, more exposure, and an expanded network of potential buyers and enthusiasts.

- **Engage regularly**: Follow influencers and collectors who are active in your area of collecting. Engage with their content by commenting, sharing, and liking their posts. Genuine interaction helps build relationships over time. For example, if you're into vintage toys, regularly participate in conversations with popular toy collectors on Instagram or YouTube.
- **Collaborate on projects**: Look for opportunities to collaborate with influencers or fellow collectors. This could be something as simple as a shared giveaway on Instagram, where you both contribute items from your collections, or as involved as a joint YouTube video where you discuss trends or unbox rare finds. These partnerships introduce you to each other's audiences and help expand your reach.
- **Feature each other's work**: Offer to feature other collectors or influencers on your social media or blog, and in return, they may feature you. For example, a shout-out from a well-known collector on their Instagram Story could lead to a sudden influx of followers for you.
- **Participate in community events**: Many online collector communities hold events such as live sales, charity auctions, or theme days (e.g., #Watch-Wednesday or #FunkoFriday on Instagram). By actively participating, you can further build your visibility and credibility.

The Benefits of Sharing Your Expertise

One of the most effective ways to build your online presence is by sharing your expertise. This not only helps others in the community but also positions you as an authority in your niche. When people see you as a trusted source of information, they're more likely to engage with your content, follow you, and even buy from you.

- **Start a blog or website**: If you have a deep knowledge of a specific type of collectible, consider starting a blog. You can share tips on caring for collectibles, guide readers on spotting fakes, or write about the history of certain items. Not only does this content help other collectors, but it also positions you as an expert in the field.

- **Create social media content**: Platforms like Instagram, YouTube, and TikTok are perfect for showing off your collection and sharing knowledge. On Instagram, you can post high-quality photos with informative captions. YouTube allows for more in-depth content—perhaps an unboxing video, a tour of your collection, or an educational series about your niche. For example, if you're a comic book collector, you might post a video explaining how to properly store and preserve valuable comics.

- **Offer advice through Q&A**: Hosting a Q&A session on Instagram Live or YouTube is a great way to interact with other collectors and showcase your expertise. Answering questions from fellow enthusiasts builds trust and makes people more likely to follow you.

- **Contribute to discussions**: Be active in online forums or social media groups related to your collectibles. Answer questions, offer advice, and share your knowledge freely. By being helpful and knowledgeable, you'll gain respect in the community, and people will begin to seek out your opinions.

- **Write reviews or guides**: Writing detailed reviews of products or guides on certain collectibles can establish you as a go-to person for reliable information. If you specialize in rare coins, for instance, reviewing a new book on the history of coin collecting or providing a beginner's guide to grading coins can attract attention from other collectors.

- **Share behind-the-scenes stories**: Collectors love a good story, so share your journey. Talk about how you got into collecting, what motivates you, and the interesting experiences you've had along the way. For instance, if you found a rare item at an unexpected place, sharing that story can make your content more relatable and engaging.

By building an online presence that is rooted in **trust, passion, and expertise**, you not only grow your reputation as a respected collector or seller but also deepen your connection to the larger collector community. This can open doors to new opportunities, whether it's expanding your sales, networking with others, or simply sharing your love of collecting with a wider audience.

6.8 Using Collector Apps and Tools

As your collection grows, keeping track of everything can feel like juggling too many balls at once. Luckily, there are **collector-specific apps** that make it much easier to manage and organize your items. These tools help you keep track of what you own, what you've sold, and what you're still hunting for—all in one place!

For example, **Gemr** is a popular app for collectors of all kinds! It allows you to catalog your items, add detailed descriptions, and even connect with other collectors. You can create categories for different parts of your collection, like vintage toys, comics, or sports memorabilia, making it easy to organize and find what you're looking for.

Another handy tool is **Collectors.com**, which is especially useful for finding items you want to add to your collection. It aggregates listings from various platforms, so you don't have to jump from website to website searching for a specific item. Imagine you're a coin collector looking for a rare 1909 Lincoln penny—you can use Collectors.com to see listings from multiple websites in one place, saving you time and effort!

For more niche collectors, there are apps designed for specific types of items. For example, if you're into Funko Pops, apps like **Stashpedia** allow you to track your collection, see what's new, and find out the value of your pops! Similarly, vintage watch collectors might use apps like **WatchBox** to organize their pieces and stay on top of the market!

These apps aren't just about tracking what you own—they also help you stay organized when buying and selling. You can keep notes on how much you paid for an item, its condition, and its market value, which is useful if you decide to sell or trade in the future.

Monitoring Market Trends with Apps

Knowing when to buy or sell is crucial for collectors, and that's where **market trend apps** come in. These apps allow you to track how the value of certain items is changing in real-time, giving you an edge when making decisions.

Take **StockX** as an example. It started as a platform for sneaker collectors, but it now includes items like trading cards and streetwear. StockX functions like a stock market for collectibles, showing you the current value of items based on recent sales. If you're a sneaker collector eyeing a limited-edition pair of Jordans, StockX can help you decide whether to buy now or wait for prices to drop.

Another great tool is **GoCollect**, which focuses on comic books. It provides real-time price guides and sales data, so you can monitor the value of your comics. Let's say you own a copy of *Amazing Fantasy #15*—the first appearance of Spider-Man. GoCollect will help you track how its value fluctuates based on recent sales, helping you determine the best time to sell or insure your investment.

These apps can also help you spot trends in the market, like when a particular item starts to become more valuable due to a resurgence in popularity. If you notice a spike in the price of vintage Pokémon cards, for instance, you might decide to sell a few before the trend fades.

By using these apps, you can stay informed and make smarter decisions about your collection, whether you're looking to expand it or cash in on your most valuable items.

6.9 The Future of Online Collecting

As technology evolves, the world of collecting is experiencing exciting developments. From digital collectibles to artificial intelligence (AI), the future of online collecting is rapidly transforming how people buy, sell, and trade items. Two major trends that are shaping the future of collecting: the rise of digital collectibles and the increasing role of technology, namely AI.

The Rise of Digital Collectibles

In recent years, digital collectibles—such as **NFTs (non-fungible tokens)**—have emerged as a new frontier for modern collectors. Unlike traditional collectibles like stamps, coins, or sports memorabilia, NFTs exist entirely in the digital world. They can be anything from digital art to virtual trading cards, each with a unique blockchain code that proves ownership and authenticity.

Platforms like **OpenSea** and **Rarible** have become hubs for buying, selling, and trading these digital assets. For instance, you might come across a limited-edition digital artwork from a famous artist or a unique moment captured in a virtual trading card (such as a highlight from a sports game). These platforms function much like eBay or Etsy, but instead of bidding on a physical object, you're buying a digital file stored on the blockchain.

One example of a booming digital collectible trend is **NBA Top Shot**, where fans can purchase, trade, and collect officially licensed NBA video highlights as NFTs. These "moments" are limited in number, and their value fluctuates based on demand, rarity, and the popularity of the player involved. For instance, a video highlight featuring LeBron James could sell for thousands of dollars, much like a rare rookie card.

While NFTs have become wildly popular in certain circles, they are also **controversial**. Some critics argue that their prices are overinflated, and the environmental impact of blockchain technology has raised concerns. Still, it's clear that digital collectibles are changing the way people think about ownership in the virtual world.

For collectors, this opens up new opportunities. You no longer need to rely on physical space to store your collection, and items are much easier to trade internationally. Imagine owning a one-of-a-kind digital art piece that you can display in a virtual gallery for people around the world to see. As NFTs continue to develop, they may become a larger part of mainstream collecting, with digital items being valued just as highly as their physical counterparts.

How AI and Technology Are Shaping the Market

The rise of **AI and advanced technologies** is also reshaping the collecting landscape in significant ways. From authenticating items to tracking market trends, these technologies are making the process of collecting more efficient, secure, and personalized.

One of the most impressive advancements in recent years is the use of AI tools for authentication. Traditionally, determining whether an item is genuine or counterfeit required expert eyes. But now, AI algorithms can scan images of items—like vintage coins, rare sports cards, or luxury watches—and analyze their authenticity by comparing them to a vast database of known originals. For example, platforms like **Entrupy** offer AI-based authentication for designer handbags, reducing the risk of buying counterfeit items online.

Another exciting development is AI-driven market analysis. Imagine you're an avid collector of vintage comic books, and you're trying to determine the best time to sell a rare issue. AI tools can track recent sales trends, analyze past data, and predict future market movements, giving you insights that would be difficult to gather on your own. This technology helps collectors make smarter decisions about when to buy, sell, or hold onto their items. Apps like **GoCollect** already offer real-time price guides and predictions for comic book collectors, based on market demand.

AI is also being used to create personalized recommendations. Much like how streaming services suggest shows or movies based on what you've watched, AI tools can suggest collectibles based on your past purchases. If you're a fan of vintage toys, an AI algorithm might recommend a rare toy from a similar era or manufacturer. This type of personalization makes it comfortaable for collectors to discover new items they didn't even know they wanted!

In addition to AI, other technologies like **augmented reality (AR)** and **virtual reality (VR)** are beginning to play a role in the collecting world. Some apps allow collectors to virtually display their collections in AR— imagine holding up your phone and seeing a rare painting or statue projected into your living room. This technology not only enhances the experience of owning a collectible but also opens up new possibilities for online showcases, where collectors can share their prized possessions with a global audience.

For example, AR is already being used by sneaker collectors to preview rare shoes "on foot" before purchasing them. Brands like **Nike** have integrated AR into their apps, allowing users to see how a sneaker looks on them without ever stepping into a store.

As AI and blockchain technology continue to evolve, the future of collecting is poised to be more dynamic, efficient, and innovative than ever before.

Whether it's using AI to ensure you're purchasing an authentic item or diving into the world of NFTs to collect digital assets, the options for collectors are expanding rapidly. As these trends grow, embracing them could offer new ways to engage with your collection and connect with a broader community of collectors from around the world.

In the future, we might see hybrid collecting, where physical items come with digital versions, or even fully virtual collections that exist only in the digital world. No matter how the landscape evolves, one thing is certain: technology is changing the rules of the game, making the act of collecting more accessible, personalized, and exciting than ever before.

Chapter 7: Notable Collectors and Iconic Collections

By now, you probably would have hunted enough treasures (i.e. collectibles, memorabilia etc.) related to your niche to proudly brand yourself as a collector and already transformed your passion for those items into a hobby that you can show off to yourself and to others as well. So, here we will go through the history and impact of famous collectors and their awesome collections as well as iconic collections that have inspired generation of collectors to embark on the journey of collecting...

7.1 The Power of Passion in Collecting

The stories of famous collectors are more than just a chronicle of the items they've gathered; they are tales of passion, dedication, and vision that have made them and their collections unforgettable! Whether it's a priceless piece of art or a seemingly mundane object, collectors have a way of elevating their chosen items into something significant that are etched in history. For novice and seasoned collectors alike, these stories can ignite inspiration, showing that collecting isn't just about acquisition—it's about creating a legacy. These individuals dedicated years or even lifetimes to their collections, building something far greater than a hobby. In doing so, they shape the very idea of what is valuable and help highlight the cultural or historical significance of their collected items.

While many collections start as simple hobbies just for the happiness of the collector, some transcend personal satisfaction to influence broader worldwide culture, history, and even the business sphere. The British Royal Collection, for example, isn't merely a gathering of personal treasures of the royals but a reflection of centuries of British history and taste and lifestyle. That's why, when you visit the The British Museum, you don't just look at pieces of history, you get to live those moments throughout the history. Likewise, individual collections often become the foundation for public institutions, like the Getty Museum or the Smithsonian, where items that once decorated private homes are now open to the whole world! These collections proves that collecting, when done with passion and purpose, can leave a lasting mark on the world, bridging the personal and the universal.

7.2 Iconic Historical Collections

The British Royal Collection

Perhaps one of the most famous historical collections globally, the British Royal Collection spans over 500,000 items, including priceless works of art, historical manuscripts, and rare jewelry. Collected over centuries, each monarch has added their touch to the collection, making it a living repository of British royal culture and history. The collection is housed across several royal residences, such as Buckingham Palace, Windsor Castle, and the Palace of Holyroodhouse, each showcasing different facets of this enormous trove of historical treasures.

One of its crown jewels, literally and figuratively, is the **Crown Jewels**—a glittering symbol of monarchy and power, featuring the **Imperial State Crown** and the **Sovereign's Orb**, which are essential pieces in coronation ceremonies. It also boasts masterpieces by **Leonardo da Vinci**, **Rembrandt**, and **Canaletto**, whose works reflect different periods of European art and influence.

More than just art, the collection contains historical relics like **Queen Victoria's sketchbooks** and personal letters exchanged between monarchs, offering an intimate glimpse into the royal family's life over the hundreds of years. It is a testament to how collections can preserve not just objects but entire epochs of human civilization—much like a time capsule of British royal heritage.

The Smithsonian Institution

If variety is the spice of life, then the Smithsonian is one of the most diverse collections in the world. With over 154 million items, it houses everything from space shuttles to the dresses of First Ladies, from ancient fossils to modern pop culture artifacts. It's a reflection of the vastness of human curiosity and achievement, where collections across disciplines come together under one umbrella.

Think about the **Apollo 11 Command Module**, which carried astronauts back from the moon, or the **Spirit of St. Louis**, Charles Lindbergh's plane, which flew across the Atlantic. These historical artifacts are preserved in the **National Air and Space Museum**, telling the story of human ambition and exploration. Then there's **Dorothy's ruby slippers** from *The Wizard of Oz*, kept in the **National Museum of American History**, which connects generations to one of Hollywood's most iconic films. The Smithsonian also houses the **Hope Diamond**, a 45.52-carat deep-blue diamond with a long history of mystery, rumored curses, and intrigue! This blend of high art, science, history, and pop culture makes the Smithsonian a true treasure chest of human achievement throughout the history.

The Vatican Museums

The Vatican Museums are a vast collections of art and artifacts, collected and curated by popes over centuries. The museums contain some of the most celebrated masterpieces in the world, including works from **Michelangelo**, **Raphael**, and **Caravaggio**, alongside ancient Roman sculptures and Egyptian mummies! The collection extends far beyond religious iconography, offering visitors a journey through the evolution of Western art and culture.

A highlight of the Vatican Museums is the **Sistine Chapel**, where Michelangelo's frescoes, particularly the iconic "Creation of Adam," continue to inspire and amaze millions. There's also **Raphael's Rooms**, including his masterpiece *The School of Athens*, which symbolizes the blend of philosophy, art, and theology. The **Gallery of Maps** showcases large, detailed ancient maps of Italy from the 16th century, painted by **Ignazio Danti**, displaying the geographical mastery of **cartographers** of the time. And for those who love antiquity, the **Gregorian Egyptian Museum** holds treasures from the land of the pharaohs, including mummies, statues, and funerary objects.

This collection reveals how the Vatican's vast artistic and cultural legacy not only preserves religious history but also fosters a deep appreciation for art and human creativity. It's a living monument to how collectors—whether individuals or institutions—can safeguard the past, ensuring that priceless works of art and history can endure the grunt of time and live on for future generations.

The Hermitage Museum, St. Petersburg

The **Hermitage Museum** in St. Petersburg, Russia, is one of the largest and oldest museums in the world, housing over 3 million items in its vast collection. Established by **Catherine the Great** in 1764, it started as her private collection of Western European art and grew into a cultural institution of immense global significance!

The Hermitage hosts a wide range of masterpieces by artists like **Michelangelo**, **Titian**, **Rubens**, and **Rembrandt**. One of its highlights is the **Peacock Clock**, a large, intricate mechanical timepiece from the 18th century that features life-sized birds in motion. The museum's collection of Scythian gold is also remarkable, representing artifacts of great archaeological value. The Hermitage spans across multiple buildings, including the **Winter Palace**, a former royal residence, which itself is a masterpiece of Baroque architecture. The Hermitage is more than just a museum; it's a palace of treasures where art, history, and imperial Russian grandeur are intertwined.

The Louvre, Paris

The **Louvre** is arguably the world's most famous museum, attracting millions of visitors every year. Once a royal palace, the Louvre now holds over 35,000 objects, ranging from prehistoric artifacts to modern art. Its star attraction is, of course, **Leonardo da Vinci's Mona Lisa**, whose enigmatic and beautiful smile has fascinated both art lovers and laymen for centuries till now. But beyond this iconic piece, the Louvre is home to countless historical and artistic treasures!

The **Venus de Milo**, an ancient Greek statue of Aphrodite (The Greek Goddess of Love and Beauty), and the **Winged Victory of Samothrace**, a Hellenistic sculpture, are just two examples of the Louvre's impressive classical antiquities collection. The museum also houses **Eugène Delacroix's** famous painting *Liberty Leading the People* and **Michelangelo's Dying Slave**, blending Renaissance artistry with political history and classical mythology. Walking through the Louvre is like taking a journey through time, as visitors encounter artifacts from ancient Egypt, Mesopotamia, Greece, and Rome, making it a cornerstone of world culture.

The Forbidden City, Beijing

The **Forbidden City** in Beijing, China, is not only an architectural marvel but also a treasure trove of Chinese imperial history. The former palace of Chinese emperors, it holds over a million pieces of art and artifacts, including jade carvings, ancient calligraphy, and porcelain. It was the home of Chinese emperors for over five centuries, from the Ming Dynasty to the end of the Qing Dynasty, and each emperor added to its collection of artistic, political and cultural items!

A notable part of its collection is the extensive number of **imperial seals**, intricately carved stones used by emperors as symbols of authority. The museum also houses ancient musical instruments, royal clothing, and elaborate **bronze vessels** from the Shang and Zhou Dynasties. One of the most unique artifacts is the **"Throne of the Son of Heaven"**, which was the seat of power for the emperor during official audiences. The Forbidden City's collection is a window into the life, culture, and politics of ancient Chinese civilization.

The Topkapi Palace Museum, Istanbul

The **Topkapi Palace Museum** in Istanbul was once the grand palace of the Ottoman sultans and is now a museum containing a rich collection of Islamic art, religious relics, and imperial treasures. Among its most revered artifacts is the **Prophet Muhammad's cloak and sword**, alongside other religious relics, which draw pilgrims and visitors from around the world. The **Imperial Treasury** holds some of the most magnificent jewels, including the **Topkapi Dagger**, encrusted with emeralds, and the famous **86-carat Spoonmaker's Diamond**.

The museum also houses a collection of delicate **Iznik ceramics**, imperial robes, and Ottoman miniatures, offering a glimpse into the lavish life of the sultans and the grandeur of the empire. With panoramic views over the Bosphorus, Topkapi Palace is not only an architectural masterpiece but a key to understanding the cultural wealth and power of the Ottoman Empire!

7.3 Famous Private Collectors

J.P. Morgan's Art and Rare Books Collection

J.P. Morgan's influence on the art world was as mighty as his financial empire. His collection was as eclectic as it was grand, ranging from **ancient Mesopotamian tablets** to the earliest printed books, such as **Gutenberg Bibles**, making his collections a blend of world history and artistic mastery. His library housed **illuminated medieval manuscripts** and original works by **Charles Dickens**, alongside paintings by **Raphael** and **Titian**. Morgan's passion for collecting wasn't driven by profit, but by a deep intellectual curiosity and passion. His dedication to rare books and fine art, preserved at the **Morgan Library & Museum**, reveals how collecting can be an intellectual pursuit—one that preserves knowledge and culture for generations. Morgan showed that even titans of industry can create legacies rooted not in wealth but in artistic and cultural enrichment.

Imelda Marcos' Shoe Collection

Imelda Marcos, the former First Lady of the Philippines, became infamous for her odd and amusing collection of over 3,000 pairs of shoes. The opulence of her collection—now housed in the **Marikina Shoe Museum**—spanned from **Salvatore Ferragamo** to **Christian Dior**, reflecting an obsession with luxury that symbolized her controversial reign! Yet beyond the extravagance, her shoes have become a metaphor for the complexity of personal collecting— how something as simple as footwear can take on deeper meanings! While her shoes drew scorn for their excess, they also serve as a reminder that collections often mirror the ambitions and insecurities of their owners, blurring the line between personal fascination and public display.

Paul Allen's Rare Art Collection

Paul Allen's stunning collection of art—one of the most valuable individual collections ever assembled—was a personal passion project that spanned eras, styles, and continents. His holdings included iconic works such as **Monet's Water Lilies** and **Gauguin's Tahitian Women**, as well as modern masterpieces like **David Hockney's Pacific Coast Highway and Santa Monica!** Allen was a true art enthusiast, and he selected each piece with careful attention according to its historical and aesthetic significance. Upon his passing, the collection was auctioned for an astounding $1.6 billion, but for Allen, it wasn't just about monetary value. His collection revealed the emotional connection between art and the individual collector, showing how art can become a deeply personal journey into history and humanity.

Peggy Guggenheim's Modern Art Collection

Peggy Guggenheim's life was as colorful as the avant-garde art she collected! Her Venice home, the **Palazzo Venier dei Leoni**, became a shrine to modern art enthusiasts, housing works from **Jackson Pollock**, **Marcel Duchamp**, and **Pablo Picasso!** Guggenheim didn't just collect; she nurtured talent, providing patronage and encouragement to some of the 20th century's most influential artists. Through her vision, she helped shape modern art as we know it! Her collection, now displayed at the **Peggy Guggenheim Collection** in Venice, exemplifies how a private passion can have a lasting public impact! Guggenheim was a trailblazer, using her wealth and status not for mere indulgence, but to revolutionize the art world and champion daring new voices.

Barbara Hutton's Jewelry Collection

Barbara Hutton, one of the world's wealthiest women, known as the **"Poor Little Rich Girl,"** had a personal life marked by tragedy but found solace in her dazzling jewelry collection. Her pieces were some of the most extraordinary and rarest in the world, including the legendary **Pasha Diamond**, the **Baroda Pearls**, and emeralds from the Maharani of Baroda, all designed by the world's finest jewelers, including **Cartier** and **Van Cleef & Arpels**. Her collection was more than a show of wealth; it was a reflection of her longing for beauty and permanence in a world that often seemed fleeting. Hutton's jewelry was a physical manifestation of her desire to hold onto something timeless, even as her personal life crumbled around her. Despite her personal struggles, her collection remains one of the most remarkable in history, a testament to the transformative power of beauty and craftsmanship.

David and Peggy Rockefeller's Art Collection

The Rockefeller name is synonymous with wealth and banking, but David and Peggy Rockefeller also became renowned for their art collection, which spanned centuries and continents. Their collection included works by **Pablo Picasso**, **Henri Matisse**, **Georges Seurat**, and **Claude Monet**, and also featured Asian ceramics and pre-Columbian art. After their deaths, the collection was auctioned off, raising over $832 million for charity, making it the most valuable collection ever sold at auction. But more than its financial value, the Rockefeller collection reflected the couple's deep engagement with art, history, and philanthropy. They weren't just collectors—they were cultural custodians, using their wealth to nurture the world's artistic heritage while giving back to society!

Steve Cohen's Contemporary Art Collection

Steve Cohen, the hedge fund billionaire, is known for his bold approach to contemporary art collecting. His collection features high-profile works by **Andy Warhol**, **Jeff Koons**, **Gerhard Richter**, and **Damien Hirst**. Perhaps the most famous piece in his collection is Hirst's **The Physical Impossibility of Death in the Mind of Someone Living**, a shark suspended in formaldehyde that challenges traditional notions of art and mortality! Cohen's collection reflects the cutting-edge, often controversial nature of contemporary art, pushing boundaries in both form and concept. His approach to collecting mirrors his career in finance—he takes risks, invests heavily, and makes bold moves! Cohen's collection is a testament to how modern collectors are not just preserving the past, but actively shaping the future of art.

Charles Saatchi's Modern Art Collection

Few collectors have had as much impact on contemporary art as **Charles Saatchi**. His support for the **Young British Artists (YBAs)**, including **Damien Hirst** and **Tracey Emin**, helped shape the trajectory of modern art in the 1990s. Saatchi's gallery in London became a launchpad for emerging talent, showcasing provocative works that captured the imagination and sometimes the outrage of the public. His ability to spot talent and take risks on controversial pieces revolutionized the art world, proving that collecting can be a form of cultural leadership. Saatchi's collection wasn't just a reflection of his taste—it was a driving force behind an entire movement, showing how collectors can actively influence the art world, rather than simply preserving it!

7.4 Iconic Pop Culture and Media Collections

George Lucas and His Star Wars Memorabilia

As the creator of *Star Wars,* one of the greatest space-sagas in the history of movies, George Lucas had a rare opportunity to amass one of the most iconic collections of film memorabilia in history. His collection includes original costumes like **Darth Vader's armor**, models of the **Millennium Falcon**, and props such as **Luke Skywalker's lightsaber**—items that are more than just film props; they are touchstones of modern mythology; and holy grail for genuine movie fanatics. For fans of the *Star Wars* universe, these objects transcend their material value, serving as physical representations of the cultural phenomenon Lucas created. His collection has not only inspired millions of fans globally but also helped build an entire subculture of collectors who seek to own a piece of that galaxy far, far away...

Elton John's Photography Collection

Elton John is not just a music icon but also a passionate collector of photography! With over 8,000 pieces in his collection, Elton's photographic treasure trove includes works by pioneering photographers like **Man Ray**, **Dorothea Lange**, and **Irving Penn**. His collection reflects his deep connection to the visual world, where each image represents a moment captured in time, much like a song. Elton once said that he's drawn to photography because it "speaks to his soul," and his passion extends across genres from early photography to cutting-edge contemporary pieces. For John, photography and music are intertwined as forms of artistic expression—one captures sound, the other captures sight, and both are a reflection of human creativity at its finest.

Steve Sansweet's Star Wars Memorabilia

Steve Sansweet, who holds the Guinness World Record for the largest private collection of *Star Wars* memorabilia, has amassed over 300,000 items, including toys, costumes, artwork, and promotional materials. His collection, housed in his personal museum **Rancho Obi-Wan** in California, has become a pilgrimage site for *Star Wars* fans! What started as a childhood fascination turned into a lifelong passion that now serves as a testament to the enduring appeal of the franchise. Sansweet's journey from fan to record-holding collector shows how a personal passion can grow into something much larger—creating a community of enthusiasts who come together to celebrate their shared love for the iconic saga!!

Quentin Tarantino's Film and Pop Culture Collection

Known for his encyclopedic knowledge of cinema, **Quentin Tarantino** is not only a filmmaker but also an avid fan and collector of film memorabilia and pop culture artifacts! His collection spans thousands of rare movie posters, prints, and obscure VHS tapes, many of which serve as inspiration for his own work. Tarantino's love of cult cinema and grindhouse films is reflected in the treasures he has accumulated over the years. He's also known for his collection of **vintage vinyl records**, a testament to his fascination with soundtracks and music's role in film. For Tarantino, these items aren't just nostalgic—they're essential tools in the creative process, helping him craft his unique cinematic vision!

Michael Jackson's Memorabilia Collection

The **King of Pop**, Michael Jackson, was also a keen collector, with his collection ranging from pop culture artifacts to rare paintings and life-sized superhero statues. His **Neverland Ranch** was filled with objects that reflected his childlike fascination with fantasy, including statues of **Superman**, **Batman**, and **Spider-Man**. Jackson also collected classic Hollywood memorabilia, including **Walt Disney's original artwork** and film costumes. His eclectic tastes extended to antique furniture and baroque-style paintings, showing how his imagination wasn't limited to the stage—it permeated his everyday life. Jackson's collection reveals a man deeply invested in preserving the wonder and magic that so often characterized his music and performances!

Debbie Reynolds' Hollywood Memorabilia Collection

Debbie Reynolds, the legendary Hollywood actress, was one of the earliest collectors to recognize the value of preserving classic Hollywood memorabilia. She amassed a huge collection of items from Hollywood's golden age, including the original **dress worn by Marilyn Monroe** in *The Seven Year Itch* and **Charlie Chaplin's bowler hat!** Reynolds saw these artifacts as an important part of American and movie culture, and she spent much of her life trying to preserve them for future generations. Her collection was eventually auctioned off for millions, but not before becoming one of the most comprehensive collections of Hollywood history, reminding us of the power of film to shape and influence global culture.

Johnny Depp's Pop Culture Art Collection

Johnny Depp, known for his eclectic and mesmerizing roles in films, is also an avid collector of pop culture and fine art. His collection includes works by **Jean-Michel Basquiat, Andy Warhol**, and **Banksy**, as well as memorabilia from his own films. Depp's love for art reflects the same eccentricity and passion that he brings to his acting career. His collection of **Basquiat paintings**, in particular, showcases his interest in artists who challenge the conventional norms of their time, much like Depp himself has done in Hollywood. His collection isn't just about investment—it's about finding art that resonates with his personal ethos and creative spirit.

7.5 Iconic Collections in Fashion and Design

Anna Wintour and Her Fashion Archive

As the editor-in-chief of *Vogue*, Anna Wintour's influence on fashion is unmatched. Her personal collection of couture spans decades of trendsetting and timeless style, reflecting her eye for elegance, luxury, and innovation. Wintour's wardrobe includes pieces from legendary designers such as **Karl Lagerfeld**, **Christian Dior**, and **Tom Ford**, each representing different eras of fashion history. Her close relationships with designers have allowed her to curate one of the most exclusive wardrobes in the world. But her collection does more than follow trends—it helps create them. Every outfit Wintour dons becomes a statement, influencing not only the runways but also the wardrobes of fashion enthusiasts worldwide. Her collection is a testament to the powerful connection between personal taste, fashion journalism, and global style.

Iris Apfel's Jewelry and Accessories

Known for her bold, eclectic style, **Iris Apfel** has turned her passion for fashion into a living art form. Her collection of jewelry and accessories is as eccentric and colorful as her personality, featuring massive statement necklaces, elaborate bangles, and uniquely patterned eyeglasses. Apfel is not interested in following traditional fashion norms; instead, she embraces maximalism, layering oversized necklaces and mixing patterns in ways that redefine the rules of style. Her collection includes vintage treasures and bespoke creations, reflecting her belief that fashion should be fun and expressive. Apfel's wardrobe, which has been showcased in exhibits, serves as an inspiring example that collecting isn't just about finding rare or expensive pieces—it's about assembling a reflection of who you are, boldly and unapologetically.

The Costume Institute's Collection at The Met

The **Costume Institute** at the Metropolitan Museum of Art in New York is a mecca for fashion lovers and historians alike. With over 33,000 pieces of clothing and accessories, the collection showcases the evolution of fashion from the 15th century to the present. Some of its most notable holdings include gowns from **Coco Chanel**, extravagant designs by **Alexander McQueen**, and couture pieces from **Yves Saint Laurent**. Each year, the Costume Institute hosts the iconic **Met Gala**, which raises funds and celebrates the world of fashion through themed exhibitions. The collection also includes historical garments such as the **Marie Antoinette-inspired gowns** and the **first-ever "New Look" dress** by **Christian Dior**. It's a reflection of how fashion evolves not just as an industry, but as an art form that tells the story of different eras and cultural movements.

Daphne Guinness and Her Avant-Garde Fashion Collection

Daphne Guinness, heiress to the Guinness family fortune, has become a modern icon in the world of avant-garde fashion. Known for her daring style, her collection includes pieces from **Alexander McQueen**, **Gareth Pugh**, and **Azzedine Alaïa**, many of which were custom-made for her. Guinness sees fashion as an extension of art, and her collection is filled with bold, sculptural garments that challenge conventional design. From towering **armadillo boots** by McQueen to elaborate **corsetry** by **Thierry Mugler**, her wardrobe reflects a deep appreciation for craftsmanship and innovation. Her collection has been featured in exhibitions, highlighting how her personal style has pushed the boundaries of fashion, transforming it into wearable art.

Victoria Beckham's High-Fashion Collection

Victoria Beckham transitioned from pop star to fashion mogul with her personal collection of high-end designer pieces, which has become the foundation of her own successful fashion brand. Her wardrobe is filled with classic, minimalist designs from **Hermès**, **Chanel**, and **Balmain**, as well as custom pieces from her own eponymous label. Beckham's collection reflects her evolution from "Posh Spice" to a respected fashion designer, and her sleek, tailored looks have made her a modern fashion icon. Her personal style and collection have not only influenced her brand but have also inspired women around the world to embrace sophistication and structure in their everyday wardrobes.

7.6 Collectors Who Changed Their Fields

Henry Ford and His Antique Car Collection

Henry Ford wasn't just an industrialist who revolutionized the automotive industry—he was also a passionate collector of antique cars and mechanical innovations. His collection, which became the centerpiece of the **Henry Ford Museum** in Dearborn, Michigan, includes not only early Ford models but also cars from across the automotive spectrum, such as the **1909 Rolls-Royce Silver Ghost** and the **1931 Bugatti Type 41 Royale**, two of the most luxurious cars ever made. Ford's collection reflects his passion for preserving the history of transportation, from early steam-powered vehicles to classic American muscle cars!

What makes Ford's collection unique is that it wasn't limited to automobiles. His museum also houses significant pieces of industrial history, such as the **Wright Brothers' original plane**, **Thomas Edison's Menlo Park laboratory**, and even the **Rosa Parks bus**, making it a collection dedicated to American ingenuity and innovation. Ford's collection helped shape how we understand the relationship between technological progress and cultural change, inspiring future generations to value history while embracing innovation.

Charles Saatchi and His Modern Art Collection

Charles Saatchi, the British advertising mogul, changed the landscape of contemporary art through his visionary collection. As an early patron of the **Young British Artists (YBAs)**, including **Damien Hirst**, **Tracey Emin**, and **Sarah Lucas**, Saatchi's collection played a pivotal role in propelling modern art into mainstream consciousness. One of the most famous pieces in his collection is Hirst's **The Physical Impossibility of Death in the Mind of Someone Living**—the iconic shark suspended in formaldehyde, a piece that encapsulated the provocative nature of the YBAs. Saatchi's collection, housed in the **Saatchi Gallery** in London, showcases his commitment to cutting-edge, often controversial art.

Saatchi didn't just collect art; he created movements. His ability to spot talent and promote emerging artists has shaped the trajectory of contemporary art, demonstrating the power of a single collector to influence an entire field. His approach also highlighted the relationship between art and commerce, as his gallery became a launchpad for many artists whose work would later fetch millions at auction. Through his collection, Saatchi turned modern art into a cultural force, proving that a collector's vision can reshape the public's understanding of art itself.

Mark Cuban's Sports Memorabilia

Billionaire Celebrity entrepreneur **Mark Cuban** has amassed an impressive collection of sports memorabilia that reflects his passion for sports and business. His collection includes everything from **autographed jerseys of NBA legends like Michael Jordan and LeBron James** to **championship rings** and game-worn gear. Cuban, who owns the **Dallas Mavericks**, uses his collection to celebrate the history and legacy of sports while also showcasing his personal connection to the world of athletics.

Cuban's collection is an example of how collecting can intersect with personal passions and business acumen. Beyond the sentimental value of each item, his memorabilia also highlights the financial and cultural significance of sports collectibles. By owning pieces of sports history, Cuban not only preserves the past but also aligns his collection with the future of sports fandom, where memorabilia continues to grow in value and importance. His approach shows that collecting isn't just about looking back—it's also about investing in a future where passion and business can thrive together, typical of a billionaire, of course!!

7.7 What We Can Learn from Famous Collectors

The common thread between all these famous collectors is passion, persistence, and vision. They weren't content to merely acquire items—they built collections with purpose. Whether they focused on art, historical artifacts, or even shoes, their dedication transformed these items into something far greater than the sum of their parts.

For instance, Henry Ford, the founder of Ford Motor Company, was not just a car manufacturer; he was also a passionate collector of Americana. His collection included everything from rare cars to antique furniture, embodying the spirit of American innovation. Ford famously established the Henry Ford Museum, which not only showcases his collection but also tells the story of American history through its artifacts, inspiring future generations to appreciate the past.

Another example is David Bowie, who, while primarily known for his music, was an avid art collector. His collection included works from contemporary artists like Damien Hirst and Jean-Michel Basquiat. Bowie's passion for art was not just a hobby; he believed in the transformative power of art to challenge norms and provoke thought, and he often used his collection as a source of inspiration for his music and performances.

For collectors, it's not just about what you collect but why? Famous collectors often follow a theme or passion, which gives their collections coherence and depth. For instance, Stephen King, the renowned author, has a penchant for collecting **vintage horror movie memorabilia**. This theme resonates with his career in horror fiction, and each piece in his collection reflects a different aspect of the genre that has influenced his writing. By building a collection with a clear purpose, you can create something meaningful that resonates with you and potentially influences others.

Similarly, Ellen DeGeneres, the beloved talk show host and comedian, is known for her collection of modern art and home decor. DeGeneres's collection is not just an accumulation of pieces; it reflects her aesthetic sensibility and her passion for design. She often showcases her collection in her home, creating a space that is both beautiful and inspirational, reminding us that our collections can serve as personal expressions of who we are.

How Famous Collectors Balance Passion and Investment

Many famous collectors find a way to balance their personal passion with the potential for financial gain. While some items are collected purely for love, others can hold strategic value, making the collection both enjoyable and profitable.

Take Paul Allen, co-founder of Microsoft and an avid art collector. His collection, which includes pieces from masters like Van Gogh and Monet, reflects his deep appreciation for art while also serving as a significant investment. Allen understood that, while his passion for art was genuine, the financial aspect could not be ignored. His collection not only enriched his life but also generated substantial returns, illustrating how passion and investment can go hand in hand.

On the other hand, Hannah D. is a contemporary sneaker collector who began her collection out of love for streetwear culture. Over the years, she has strategically focused on limited-edition releases and collaborations with famous designers, turning her passion into a profitable venture. By staying informed about trends and leveraging her connections in the sneaker community, Hannah has managed to curate a collection that not only reflects her identity but also appreciates significantly in value.

Understanding this balance is key to turning a hobby into a lasting legacy! As these collectors demonstrate, a successful collection is not merely about the items themselves; it's about the stories they tell, the passions they reflect, and the connections they foster.

Chapter 8: The Emotional Side of Collecting

Collecting is more than just a hobby; it's an emotional journey throughout life's ups and downs! It takes us on a rollercoaster ride filled with nostalgia, discovery, and personal growth. The things we gather over time are more than objects—they are reflections of who we are, where we've been, and what we hold dear. Let's explore the emotional layers of collecting, understanding how this seemingly simple activity taps into the deepest parts of our hearts and minds.

8.1 The Connection Between Collecting and Emotion

At the core of every collection is a story—a personal connection that draws the collector to those particular items. Whether it's vintage comic books, rare vinyl records, or antique furniture, the impulse to collect is often driven by deep psychological and emotional needs!

For many, collecting is rooted in nostalgia. The desire to recapture a moment from childhood or reconnect with a piece of the past motivates people to gather items that trigger fond memories. Imagine holding an old toy that you once loved as a child—the touch of it in your hand can transport you back to simpler and playful times, like a time machine wrapped in plastic!

But nostalgia is just one piece of the puzzle. Collecting also fulfills a need for self-expression. The things we choose to collect say something about who we are! It's an intimate form of curation, where each item is a piece of a larger narrative, showcasing our passions, tastes, and even our quirks.

For some collectors, collecting becomes a way to build connection—to a community, a period in history, or even an era they never lived through. A person might never have experienced the 1950s firsthand, but their love of retro fashion or mid-century modern furniture helps them connect to that time!

The Role of Sentimentality

Sentimentality is a powerful driving force in collecting. The objects we gather often carry emotional weight, tied to important people, places, or experiences. A photograph from a family vacation, a watch inherited from a grandparent, or a postcard from a long-lost friend—all these items have stories etched into them, making them far more valuable than their monetary worth.

Consider a collector of old vinyl records. Each album may be linked to a memory—dancing in the living room with a partner, listening to a favorite song with friends, or even finding comfort in music during difficult times. These items become keepsakes of emotional milestones, reminding us not just of the music but the moments shared while it played.

8.2 Collecting as a Form of Identity

A collection can be a mirror, reflecting back a person's identity. The specific items we gather, whether it's rare stamps or art prints, offer insights into our personalities, values, and interests. Every collection is a unique fingerprint, revealing layers of who we are, often in ways that words cannot.

Take, for instance, a person who collects travel souvenirs. Their shelves might be filled with small trinkets from all over the world, each representing a different adventure. To them, those items are more than mementos—they're markers of where they've been, what they've experienced, and the parts of themselves they discovered along the way.

Collections are like wardrobes for the soul, each item a chosen garment that says, "This is who I am!"

Building Community Through Shared Interests

One of the most fulfilling aspects of collecting is the community it creates. Collectors, no matter what they specialize in, often find others who share their passion. These connections form the basis of friendships and camaraderie, built around the love of a shared interest.

Collectors' fairs, conventions, and online forums are filled with people bonding over rare finds, swapping stories, and offering advice. It's a space where people from different walks of life come together, united by a common hobby. In this way, collecting offers more than material rewards—it provides a sense of belonging. Whether it's a group of coin collectors marveling over rare currencies or action figure enthusiasts trading stories of childhood heroes, shared passions build strong emotional ties!

8.3 Nostalgia and Memory in Collecting

Nostalgia is a time machine in disguise. It pulls us back to moments that shaped us, allowing us to relive our favorite memories. Collecting is a natural extension of this, offering a way to capture and hold onto the past.

A person might collect items from their childhood—old toys, movie posters, or memorabilia from their favorite sports team whenever they get the chance. These items are imbued with meaning far beyond their physical form. Holding them can conjure the sights, sounds, and feelings of a bygone era, transporting the collector back to a version of themselves that still feels familiar.

Many collectors think not just about the here and now, but also about the future. A well-curated collection is often seen as a legacy—something to be passed down to future generations. It's a way to preserve memories, tastes, and passions, leaving behind a personal narrative told through objects.

In this sense, collections become heirlooms and legacy, carefully maintained and cherished so they can tell their and their collector's stories long after the collector is gone.

8.4 Coping with Loss and Emotional Challenges

For a dedicated collector, losing an item can feel like a personal tragedy! Whether it's due to theft, damage, or the need to sell, the emotional toll can be profound. Collections are often more than the sum of their parts; each item holds sentimental value, acting as a physical reminder of a memory, a moment, or even a person! When one of these objects is lost, it can feel like a small piece of the collector's identity is slipping away.

It's important to recognize that for collectors, objects become emotional anchors. The loss of a cherished item might stir up feelings similar to those experienced when losing a family heirloom or even a beloved pet. Just as a photograph may remind us of a loved one or a place long past, a rare coin or a signed first edition can evoke memories of the moment it was discovered, the people involved, or the journey to obtain it. These objects are wrapped in layers of personal history, making their loss all the more poignant.

When collectors lose an item, the grief can manifest in different ways. Some may feel frustration at the randomness of theft or accidents, while others might feel regret or guilt if they were forced to sell an item. The emotions tied to these events are real, and it's important to give space to those feelings, much like mourning the loss of something deeply personal.

Recovering from such a loss involves acceptance—recognizing that while the item may be gone, the memories it represented remain intact. Some collectors find solace in sharing stories about their lost items with other collectors, turning grief into an opportunity to bond with others who understand the emotional value of their collections.

Balancing Passion and Financial Realities

While collecting can bring immense joy, it's also a hobby that can come with financial challenges. The pursuit of rare or valuable items can lead to financial strain, particularly when collections grow larger or the price of sought-after pieces climbs. For some collectors, the cost of maintaining and expanding their collections can begin to outweigh the emotional satisfaction they bring, leading to difficult choices.

Financial pressures can sometimes force collectors into a corner where they must consider selling parts of their collections to stay afloat. This decision often creates emotional conflict! For someone who has spent years accumulating a collection, letting go of even a single item can feel like betraying his passion. The process of selling is rarely just a financial transaction—it's an emotional one, too. Each sale might feel like a loss, not just of the item but of the memories and stories attached to it.

There's also the uncertainty of value in collecting. While some items might appreciate over time, others may not. A collector may have invested time, energy, and money into acquiring a piece, only to find that its market value has stagnated or dropped. This can lead to feelings of disappointment, as the financial realities clash with the emotional connection to the items!

For many, the balancing act between passion and practicality is a delicate one. It's not just about money—it's about weighing the joy and fulfillment of collecting against the potential stress of financial strain. The key lies in setting realistic expectations. Collecting should be an enriching experience, not a financial burden. By regularly reassessing one's financial situation and the goals of their collection, collectors can navigate this balancing act with more clarity.

When financial hardship necessitates downsizing, it's important for collectors to remember that their passion is not defined by the number of items they possess but by the stories and experiences they've accumulated along the way. Selling an item doesn't erase its emotional significance or the joy it once brought. In fact, some collectors find freedom in streamlining their collections, focusing on quality over quantity, and appreciating what remains even more deeply.

By maintaining a healthy perspective, collectors can ensure that their love for collecting remains a source of joy and not a source of stress. Ultimately, it's the passion, the hunt, and the connections forged along the way that matter most—not the final tally of collectibles on a shelf.

8.5 The Therapeutic Benefits of Collecting

For many, collecting offers much more than the simple joy of gathering items—it becomes a form of therapy, mental peace, a way to process emotions and find peace in the midst of life's challenges! In a world that can often feel overwhelming, the act of collecting, rather any hobby, creates a personal refuge, a corner of the universe where things can be neatly categorized, displayed, enjoyed and understood. This sense of control and structure can be deeply comforting, especially when other parts of life feel chaotic or uncertain!

The therapeutic value of collecting lies in its ability to bring focus and mindfulness. The careful research, the thrill of discovery, and the satisfaction of curating a collection all require a high degree of attention to detail. This level of engagement encourages mindfulness, helping collectors to stay grounded in the present moment. Whether it's meticulously organizing a bookshelf of first editions or cataloging vintage vinyl records, the act of focusing entirely on a task can provide a much-needed mental break from daily stresses. It's a form of active meditation, where the mind can rest and reset while still being engaged.

In the fast-paced modern world, where instant gratification is the norm, collecting slows things down. It teaches patience and dedication, reminding us that good things take time and effort. The search for a rare item or the process of completing a collection can span years, offering long-term satisfaction that's far deeper than a quick impulse purchase. In this way, collecting offers a form of emotional nourishment, providing lasting fulfillment rather than fleeting pleasure.

Stories of Healing Through Collecting

There are countless stories of individuals who have found healing through their journey as a collector, especially during times of grief, loneliness, or personal upheaval. One such story is of a man I knew about in a collector's community, who, after the sudden loss of a loved one, began collecting vintage postcards from cities and places they had once visited together. Each postcard became a way to honor the memories they had shared, preserving the places they'd been in a tangible form. For him, the act of collecting wasn't just about acquiring items—it was a means of keeping his connection to those experiences alive, even as life moved forward without his loved one!

In another instance, a female collector I know was coping with the end of a long-term relationship found solace in collecting old cameras. Each camera represented a different era of photography, a symbol of the different chapters of her life. Through the lens of her collection, she began to see beauty in the past and excitement for the future!

Collecting can be a pathway to reclaiming control during difficult times. For someone dealing with anxiety or depression, it can serve as a reliable routine—

a steady, comforting activity that brings small but significant joys. It's a way of bringing order to emotional chaos, offering a sense of predictability and satisfaction in a world that often feels uncertain.

Beyond individual healing, collectors often share their stories with others, creating a sense of community and connection. Whether it's through online forums, social media, or local meetups, collectors bond over their shared passions, offering support and understanding. These connections can provide a sense of belonging, especially for those who might otherwise feel isolated! The shared language of collecting becomes a bridge, linking people across different backgrounds, experiences, and stages of life.

Collecting, in these instances, is about more than just amassing objects. It becomes a form of emotional expression, a way to process difficult feelings, and a tool for personal growth. The things we collect are often reflections of what we value, and the journey of building a collection can be a journey of healing, self-discovery, and even transformation!

8.6 The Dark Side of Collecting

Obsessive Collecting and Hoarding

While collecting can be a profound source of happiness, satisfaction, and even emotional healing, it's essential to accept that it can also slip into unhealthy territory! When the desire to collect transforms into an obsession, the once-joyful pursuit can become a source of anxiety, stress, and emotional strain. The fine line between passionate collecting and obsessive hoarding is often difficult to see until it's crossed—and by then, the emotional and psychological toll can be heavy!

Collecting, at its best, is a balanced act of curation, where each item is thoughtfully selected and cherished. However, when the act of acquiring overtakes the joy of ownership, collectors can find themselves overwhelmed by the sheer volume of their possessions. Rather than feeling fulfilled, the obsessive collector may feel trapped by their collection, surrounded by clutter and chaos. The items that were once carefully chosen can begin to lose their meaning, replaced by a compulsion to gather more, regardless of necessity or space.

This can lead to hoarding, where the pursuit of new items becomes relentless and unchecked, often driven by an irrational fear of missing out or losing something important. The emotional weight of such a collection can be heavy. Instead of bringing joy, it creates stress and anxiety—each new item adding to a mountain of possessions that no longer feels manageable. Rooms may fill with boxes, shelves may sag under the weight, and what once brought pleasure now causes tension, straining relationships and personal well-being.

The transition from collecting to hoarding is not always easy to recognize. It can start with innocent acquisitions that seem harmless—another book, another figurine, another antique. But as the collection grows, so does the emotional attachment to the act of acquiring. The collector may begin to lose sight of why they started collecting in the first place, as the obsession for more takes precedence over the meaning behind each piece.

The emotional toll is multiplied by the difficulty in letting go! Obsessive collectors may find it incredibly hard to part with any of their items, regardless of their condition or relevance to the original collection. This attachment can stem from a fear of loss, of losing a piece of themselves, or from the belief that an item might somehow be needed in the future. The anxiety of letting go can be paralyzing, leaving the collector trapped by the very items they once treasured.

Emotional Burden of Incomplete Collections

Another common challenge in the darker side of collecting is the emotional burden of incompleteness. For many collectors, the drive to find that one elusive piece can become an all-consuming mission. The dream of completing a set or acquiring a rare item can create an emotional tension that hovers over every aspect of their lives. While collecting is often about the journey rather than the destination, the unfulfilled goal of a perfect or complete collection can become a heavy emotional weight to bear.

The frustration of endless searching can leave collectors feeling exhausted and disillusioned. The constant pursuit can overshadow the enjoyment of the items they already possess, shifting focus from appreciating what they have to stressing over what they don't. This obsession with completing a collection can start to feel like chasing a mirage, always just out of reach, creating an emotional pressure cooker.

For some, the pressure to complete a collection becomes more intense due to external factors—comparing oneself to other collectors, social media "collection envy," or attending conventions where others proudly display their complete sets. These comparisons can lead to feelings of inadequacy, as collectors may begin to question the value of their own collections if they aren't as "complete" or as valuable as others'. Instead of finding joy in their unique collection, they may feel a growing sense of dissatisfaction, constantly measuring themselves against an unattainable ideal.

This emotional burden can also manifest in more subtle ways. Some collectors may feel compelled to stretch their financial limits, spending money they can't afford on an item just to complete a set or achieve a goal. This can create a cycle of emotional highs and lows—excitement when a new piece is acquired, followed by guilt or regret when the financial implications sink in.

The journey to complete a collection can become a psychological trap—a constant reminder of what is missing rather than a celebration of what has been found. And while the thrill of the hunt is part of the joy of collecting, when it turns into an obsessive need to complete, it robs the experience of its meaning and fulfillment.

8.7 Finding Balance in Collecting

To truly enjoy the rewards of collecting, it's essential to establish healthy boundaries. Without a limit, the pursuit of new items can quickly spiral into an overwhelming endeavor. Setting limits doesn't diminish the passion—it protects it! A balanced approach to collecting allows enthusiasts to savor their finds, appreciate what they have, and avoid turning their love of collecting into a source of stress or anxiety.

The first step in maintaining balance is understanding when to stop. This can mean different things for different collectors. For some, it might be a physical limit, such as not allowing their collection to exceed the available display or storage space. For others, it's a financial cap—deciding ahead of time how much they are willing or able to spend on their hobby each month. The act of limiting the collection doesn't restrict the joy of it; instead, it adds focus and clarity, ensuring that each new piece is meaningful and well-considered!

Regularly taking stock of one's collection can also provide a helpful reality check. A simple self-reflection—"Is this still bringing me joy? Am I collecting with intention, or am I just accumulating for the sake of it?"—can help collectors ensure their passion remains a positive force in their lives. By periodically reassessing, collectors can make thoughtful decisions about what to keep, what to let go, and how to proceed without feeling overwhelmed.

Another critical aspect of setting healthy boundaries is understanding motivations. Collectors should ask themselves why they are drawn to a particular item or genre. Is it out of genuine interest and love, or is it driven by external pressures, like trends or a desire for status? By getting to the root of their motivations, collectors can realign their actions with their true passions, ensuring that the hobby enriches their lives rather than becoming a burden.

In a world that celebrates more, bigger, and faster, setting boundaries might feel counterintuitive. But, like in any relationship, including the one between a collector and their collection, balance and moderation are the keys to long-term fulfillment. Healthy boundaries not only protect collectors from burnout but also ensure that each item added brings joy rather than stress.

Creating Meaningful Experiences

While collecting is often focused on acquiring physical items, the true beauty of the hobby lies in the experiences it creates! These experiences are what turn a simple possession into a cherished memory, elevating the act of collecting from a material pursuit to something more emotionally and socially fulfilling.

The joy of collecting isn't just in owning an item—it's in the stories we create around it… Imagine attending a collectors' convention and stumbling upon that one rare piece you've been hunting for years. The excitement of the find is not just about the object itself, but also about the journey that led you there—the people you met along the way, the knowledge you gained, and the experiences you shared with other enthusiasts. Each piece in a collection is like a bookmark in the story of your life, marking moments of discovery, learning, and connection.

Sharing collections with friends and fellow collectors adds another layer of meaning. Whether it's through showing off your rarest baseball cards, inviting friends over to admire your carefully arranged vinyl records, or participating in online collector communities, sharing your collection allows you to connect with others who share your passion. These interactions often create lasting friendships and a sense of belonging, turning what could be a solitary activity into a communal experience. In this way, collecting becomes less about the objects themselves and more about the relationships that form around them.

Attending conventions or joining meetups dedicated to niche-based collecting can be especially rewarding. These events offer collectors a chance to engage with others who understand the intricacies and emotions tied to their particular hobby. It's not just about buying, selling, or trading items—it's about connecting with like-minded individuals, swapping stories, learning from experts, and deepening your appreciation for your collection. Being part of a community can breathe new life into a collector's journey, making it richer and more meaningful.

Even in the digital age, there are countless ways to make collecting more about connection than acquisition. Virtual forums, social media groups, and online auctions all offer ways for collectors to share their expertise, seek advice, and celebrate milestones with people from around the world. In these spaces, collectors can discuss their passions, debate the finer points of their hobby, and build relationships that might never have been possible in a pre-digital world.

Ultimately, while the items themselves are valuable, it's the experiences and connections that transform a collection into something much more profound. By focusing on these experiences—whether through shared moments, community involvement, or personal milestones—collectors can ensure that their hobby remains a source of joy, meaning, and personal fulfillment for years to come, not a business venture where they just hoard collectibles or memorabilia for their monetary value. Instead of just filling shelves or display cases, these objects fill their lives with stories, connections, and a sense of purpose that goes far beyond the physical objects they collect.

Chapter 9: Passing on Your Collection

9.1 The Importance of Planning for the Future

As a collector, the passion, energy, and resources you've poured into your collection have likely built it into something remarkable—something far greater than just the sum of its parts. Whether your collection is filled with antique coins, rare stamps, vintage toys, retro games, or fine art, there comes a point where you need to ask yourself: What happens to it when I'm no longer around?

It might seem like a far-off concern, but planning for the future of your collection is as important as curating it. Without a plan, the collection could be at risk of being divided, sold off without any context, or even forgotten from history! By taking the time to plan now, you're not just protecting the monetary value of your items; you're also safeguarding the emotional and historical significance of your life's work. Planning ahead ensures that your collection's story continues, even after you're no longer there to tell it.

A well-curated collection reflects your unique interests, experiences, and perspective. In many ways, it's a personal legacy—an extension of who you are as a person! By thoughtfully planning how to pass on your collection, you can ensure that your passion continues to resonate with others, even long after you've left it behind.

Imagine a beautifully crafted watch passed down through generations. Each wearer isn't just donning a piece of fine craftsmanship; they're carrying a bit of history, a thread that ties them to the original collector's love for timepieces. Or picture a museum display of rare maps that once belonged to a private collector—the public now able to explore geography's past thanks to one person's dedicated effort. This is the power of a collection's legacy.

9.2 Options for Passing on Your Collection

Family Heirloom: Passing It to Loved Ones

For many collectors, the most meaningful and emotionally accurate option is to keep the collection within the family. Passing it to children, grandchildren, or close friends can ensure that the collection remains cherished and appreciated by those you hold dear. However, this approach requires more than just handing over a box of items. It's important to make sure the recipient understands the collection's significance. It can be a wonderful opportunity to share stories, memories, and insights that have made the collection so valuable to you. Also it'd be a way for your legacy to be passed on to your future generation through the treasures you've collected!

Donating to Museums or Institutions

Another option to consider is donating your collections to a museum, library, or institution. This ensures the collection is preserved and shared with the public, allowing future generations to learn from and enjoy it. If your collection has historical or educational value, this could be the perfect option! Working with curators can help guarantee that the collection is handled with care and displayed in a way that honors its significance. Whether it's a collection of rare manuscripts or vintage comic books, the right institution can become a fitting home. And as a collector, you can get worldwide recognition and fame by literally collecting objects that feel passionate about.

Selling Your Collection

Some collectors choose to sell their collection, either while they're still alive or as part of their estate plan. This can be an opportunity to ensure that the collection finds new homes with people who share the same passion! Selling can also help secure a financial legacy for your heirs. Understanding the process—whether through auctions, dealers, or private sales—can help you navigate the complexities of liquidating a collection while ensuring that it goes to the right buyers.

9.3 Passing on Your Collection to Future Generations

Getting younger generations interested in your collection can be a challenge, especially in this era where digital distractions are rampant among not only young people but also older generation. But the key to sparking interest lies in the underlying interesting stories behind the items. A collection isn't just a group of objects; it's a narrative. Share the stories behind each item—why you acquired it, where it came from, what makes it unique! This personal connection can help kindle curiosity and create a sense of ownership among younger family members as well as spark an interest in your collector's adventures in them.

Teaching Responsibility for the Collection

If you're passing on your collection, it's important to ensure that the next generation knows how to care for it properly. This goes beyond simply handing over the items. Teaching them about preservation techniques, from maintaining old books to storing delicate fabrics, is crucial. Explain the importance of documentation, condition reports, and regular upkeep. If they're to be custodians of the collection, they need to be equipped with the knowledge to protect its value and legacy. Who knows? Maybe one of your offspring might spark an interest in collecting and you get a chance to pass the baton.

Ensuring Your Collection's Future Care

One way to ensure your collection's future care is through legal measures such as setting up a trust or endowment. This can provide resources for the collection's long-term preservation, whether through a museum or private foundation. Including specific instructions in your will can also help ensure that your collection is handled exactly as you wish, from how it's displayed to how it's passed on.

9.4 Legal and Financial Considerations

Including Your Collection in Your Will

A collection that's left out of a will can lead to disputes, confusion, and sometimes even the loss of valuable items. To avoid this, it's essential to include detailed instructions in your estate plan. Specifically declare who should inherit the collection and outline any special wishes regarding its future, such as whether it should be kept together or sold off. This clarity ensures that your collection is handled according to your wishes and avoids unnecessary conflicts!

Estate Taxes and Legal Challenges

Passing on a valuable collection can have tax implications, and without careful planning, these taxes can reduce the inheritance significantly. Consult with legal and financial advisors to minimize tax burdens and ensure a smooth transfer. This might involve gifting items before death, donating for tax deductions, or setting up trusts…

Creating Trusts and Foundations

If your collection is particularly significant, you might consider establishing a trust or foundation specifically for its preservation! This not only ensures its care but also provides opportunities for public exhibition, research, and education. A well-planned foundation can preserve the collection's legacy long after you're gone.

9.5 Donating Your Collection

Choosing the Right Institution

Donating your collection to an institution can be a meaningful way to ensure that it remains accessible to the public as well as appreciated by them and is preserved for future generations. However, choosing the right institution is crucial! Your collection deserves to be housed somewhere that understands its significance, where it will be valued for its overall purpose and cared for in the way you intended.

Start by researching museums, universities, or libraries that specialize in the type of items you've collected. If your collection is focused on a specific niche—like rare fossils or vintage photography—look for institutions with related departments in those institutions. Once you've narrowed it down, arrange meetings with curators or collections managers to discuss your donation. It's important to find out how they intend to use the collection: Will it be displayed? Archived? Are there guarantees it won't be sold off or forgotten? Finding the right home for your precious collections ensures your collection's story continues to be told in the right context...

The Donation Process

Once you've selected an institution, the donation process begins with formal discussions about the terms and conditions. These discussions might include whether the collection will be donated in full or in parts, any preferences you have about how the items are used, and even whether your name will be associated with the donation for future exhibits or research.

The process often involves signing legal agreements that clearly outline the institution's responsibilities for the care, display, or archival of the collection! Some institutions may even allow you to be involved in setting up the initial exhibits or provide opportunities for educational programs that reflect your expertise and passion.

Tax Benefits of Donation

Donating a collection can offer significant tax benefits. In many countries, donations to recognized charitable institutions may be tax-deductible, providing an attractive incentive for collectors with valuable assets. If your collection has a substantial market value, these deductions could help offset estate taxes, making the process financially beneficial for you or your heirs.

Consult with a tax professional who understands the specifics of art, antiques, or historical object donations. They'll help you navigate the paperwork and ensure you maximize these benefits while staying compliant with tax laws. Donation can be a win-win: preserving your collection's legacy while offering you financial relief!

9.6 Selling Your Collection

Timing is everything when it comes to selling a collection. The market's ups and downs can significantly affect the value of your items, so it's essential to stay informed about trends. For example, certain items may be more desirable during anniversaries or resurgence of interest in a particular era or artist. A vintage car collection might fetch higher prices if classic car shows or documentary featuring those models bring them back into the spotlight.

On the other hand, some collectors prefer to sell while they are still alive to ensure their treasures find the right homes and they have control over the process. This approach can offer both financial rewards and personal satisfaction, knowing the collection will be cared for.

Choosing the Right Auction House or Dealer

Selling a collection is not as simple as posting it online. The right auction house or dealer can make all the difference in getting the best price and ensuring the collection's integrity. Auction houses like Sotheby's or Christie's have dedicated departments for specific types of items, offering a vast network of buyers with deep appreciation for what you've collected.

Alternatively, working with dealers—whether local or international—might provide more flexibility. Dealers often have established relationships with private collectors and can negotiate sales directly. Each option comes with its pros and cons: auctions typically have fees, but the global exposure can lead to higher sale prices, while private dealers might offer quicker, more intimate sales but at lower margins!

Preparing for Auction or Sale

If you decide to sell your collection through an auction or a dealer, preparation is key. Professional appraisals, cleaning or restoring items, and proper documentation will enhance the appeal of your collection. For instance, a rare painting accompanied by its provenance or a historical artifact linked to its original context will fetch a higher price.

When creating listings or auction catalog entries, focus on the unique aspects of your collection that set it apart. Stories or historical details can capture buyers' imaginations, helping to secure higher bids. Preparing your collection professionally, well in advance of the sale allows you to present it at its best, ensuring you receive the recognition (and financial reward) it deserves!

9.7 Managing the Emotional Aspects of Letting Go

Letting go of a collection, whether through sale or donation, can be deeply emotional. For years or decades, these items have been an integral part of your life, source of your enjoyment, representing not only a hobby but memories, adventures, and a personal journey. It's natural to feel conflicted about parting with them.

This emotional attachment can sometimes make it difficult to make objective decisions. Selling might feel like losing a part of yourself, while donating could bring up concerns about whether the items will be appreciated in the same way you did. It's important to take time to process these feelings. Many collectors find peace in knowing that, even if they no longer own the collection, it will continue to bring joy or education to others. Letting go doesn't mean erasing your connection to these items—it means allowing them to live on beyond your ownership.

Creating a Legacy Beyond Ownership

One way to navigate the emotional complexities of letting go is by focusing on the legacy your collection will leave behind. Whether displayed in a museum, sold to an appreciative new collector, or passed down through your family as heirloom, your collection can continue to impact people beyond your personal ownership.

Think of yourself as a steward rather than an owner. Your role in building, curating, and preserving the collection is just one chapter in its long story.

Honoring the Stories Behind the Collection

One of the most significant ways to pass on your collection is by preserving and compiling the stories behind the items. Even as you part with the physical pieces, the stories can remain as part of your personal legacy. Documenting the personal connections, the hunt, or the joy behind each item can enrich its value for future owners or curators.

Consider creating a written or digital record of your collection's history and cultural significance. These stories can be shared with your family, institutions, or new collectors. This personal context makes the collection more meaningful and empowers the other person to preserve its emotional value, even after it has been passed on!

9.8 Creating a Digital Archive of Your Collection

In a world that's increasingly digital, creating a digital archive of your collection is not just an option—it's an essential part of preserving its legacy. A digital archive can serve as a permanent record of your collection, making it accessible to future generations, whether or not the physical items remain together.

Digitizing your collection involves more than just taking photos. It's about creating detailed records, including descriptions, provenance, historical significance, and personal anecdotes about each item. This can be shared with future generations, researchers, or even potential buyers, ensuring the collection's story is open to the world no matter where the physical items end up.

Sharing Your Digital Archive with Future Generations

Once your collection is digitized, you have the option of sharing it with family members, scholars, or even the public. You might consider creating a private family archive or posting the collection online through platforms like social media, where others can appreciate your passion and expertise. For collectors of rare or unique items, an online presence can even spark a broader interest in your field, contributing to its appreciation and study long after your collection has been passed on.

How to digitize properly?

Digitizing your collection is an essential way to preserve, organize, and share it with others. Doing it properly ensures that both the images and information about your items are clear, accessible, and secure for future generations. Below are the steps and best practices for properly digitizing a collection:

1. Create an Inventory of Your Collection

Before you start digitizing, you need to organize and document your collection. This includes:

- **Categorizing**: Organize items into categories (e.g., paintings, documents, stamps, etc.).
- **Labeling**: Assign a unique identifier to each item (a number or code) for easy reference.
- **Describing**: Write descriptions of each item, including details like origin, date of acquisition, material, size, and any unique characteristics.
- **Recording Provenance**: Include any historical or personal significance, and document how you acquired each item.

2. Select the Right Equipment

Using the proper tools ensures high-quality digital records:

- **High-Resolution Camera or Scanner**: For documents, books, and flat objects, a high-resolution scanner (at least 300 dpi for documents, 600-1200 dpi for photos) is ideal. For three-dimensional objects (e.g., figurines or sculptures), use a high-resolution camera with good lighting.
- **Lighting Setup**: Use diffuse lighting to avoid harsh shadows and reflections, especially for glossy or shiny items like coins or artwork behind glass.
- **Tripod or Scanning Platform**: If using a camera, a tripod helps ensure stability, allowing you to capture sharp, focused images consistently. For small objects, a scanning platform is helpful.

3. Capture High-Quality Images

- **Resolution Matters**: Ensure that images are of high enough resolution to capture fine details. Aim for at least 300 DPI for most objects and higher for small or detailed items like stamps or jewelry.
- **Multiple Angles**: For 3D items, take photos from multiple angles to capture the full form of the object. Document the front, back, sides, and any noteworthy details.
- **File Formats**: Save images in high-quality formats like TIFF for long-term archival purposes. JPEG is acceptable for sharing or uploading but

always retain a master image in a lossless format (e.g., TIFF).

4. Create Detailed Metadata

Metadata is the information that describes your collection in a digital format. Proper metadata ensures that you, or anyone else, can understand and manage the digital archive easily. It should include:

- **Title**: A simple, clear title for each item.
- **Date**: The year the item was created or collected.
- **Dimensions**: The size or weight of the item.
- **Description**: Any relevant information about the item's history, cultural significance, or personal connection to it.
- **Condition**: Document any damage, wear, or repairs the item has undergone.
- **Keywords**: Add tags or keywords to make items easier to search for in the future.

5. Organize and Store Your Digital Files

A structured and consistent storage system is crucial for easy access and long-term preservation:

- **Folder Structure**: Organize your files in folders by category, year, or collection type. For example, you could use folders like "Vintage Toys > 1960s > Model Cars" to keep everything in order.
- **File Naming**: Use a clear and consistent naming convention. For example, "ToyCar_1962_Model01_FrontView" is more useful than "IMG_00123.jpg." Include the item's unique identifier in the file name for easy cross-referencing with your inventory.
- **Backup Regularly**: Use external hard drives or cloud storage to back up your digital files. Multiple backups, stored in different locations, will protect your data from accidental loss or damage.
- **Cloud Solutions**: Consider using a dedicated cloud storage service (like Google Drive, Dropbox, or specialized archive platforms) to store and

share your collection securely.

6. Create a Digital Archive

- **Digital Database**: Use a software solution to catalog and manage your digital collection. There are specialized programs like **CollectiveAccess**, **PastPerfect**, or even **Excel** and **Google Sheets** for smaller collections.
- **Include Scans and Metadata**: Link each image file with its corresponding metadata in your digital database. If you have detailed provenance or personal stories, store them along with the image so future generations can understand the full context.

7. Consider Digital Preservation Formats

As technology evolves, file formats and storage media can become obsolete. To prevent this, follow these digital preservation best practices:

- **Use Open or Standard Formats**: Open formats like TIFF, PDF/A, and plain text are more likely to remain accessible in the future. Avoid proprietary formats that may be hard to open as software changes.
- **Regularly Update and Convert Files**: Check your files every few years to ensure they're still accessible. Update storage media and convert files to newer formats if necessary.

8. Sharing Your Digital Collection

Once your collection is digitized, sharing it can be a great way to spread the joy and knowledge behind it:

- **Social Media and Websites**: Platforms like Instagram, Pinterest, or dedicated collection-sharing sites (like **Flickr** or **Behance**) can be used to display your items to a broader audience.
- **Family Sharing**: If your goal is to share with family members, you can create private galleries using services like Google Photos or shared cloud drives.

- **Public Archives and Research Libraries**: If your collection is of historical or educational significance, consider partnering with online databases or digital libraries that specialize in collections like yours.

9. Using Advanced Technology for Provenance and Security

New technologies are emerging that can add layers of security and provenance to your digital collection:

- **Blockchain**: Using blockchain to store provenance and ownership information can ensure that future owners and historians have an unchangeable, verified record of an item's history.
- **NFTs (Non-Fungible Tokens)**: For digital art or collections, NFTs can be used to verify ownership and create a permanent digital record associated with the item.

10. Legal and Copyright Considerations

If your collection includes items you created or intellectual property, consider the legal implications of sharing them digitally:

- **Copyright**: Ensure you own the rights to items you digitize, especially if they'll be shared publicly.
- **Licensing**: You may choose to apply licenses (such as Creative Commons) to your digital archives, specifying how others can use the images or information.

By following these steps, you can properly digitize your collection, creating a high-quality, organized digital archive that preserves the integrity, value, and history of your items for generations to come.

9.9 Ensuring Your Collection's Future

Planning for Long-Term Preservation

The long-term care of a collection requires foresight. Whether your collection consists of delicate textiles, rare books, or historical artifacts, proper preservation is essential to maintaining its value and integrity over time. You might consider setting aside funds specifically for the upkeep of the collection, either through a trust or in collaboration with a museum that specializes in conservation.

Proper storage, regular maintenance, and controlled environments can all play a role in ensuring that your collection lasts for decades to come. Consulting with preservation experts can help you develop a plan that addresses the specific needs of your items, ensuring that they're protected from environmental damage, decay, or mishandling.

Trusting Others with Your Legacy

Ultimately, passing on your collection is an act of trust. Whether you entrust it to family members, an institution, or a buyer, you're placing your faith in others to continue what you've started. And that's a positive step—a way of sharing your passion with the world.

Trusting others with your collection doesn't mean relinquishing control. It means accepting that the value of a collection lies not just in its ownership, but in its ability to inspire and educate. With careful planning and thoughtful decisions, your collection can continue to impact future generations, telling stories, preserving history, and sparking curiosity, even after you've passed it on.

Conclusion: The Ongoing Journey of a Collector

Collecting is not just a pastime or a hobby or a simple act of acquiring objects—it's a journey, one that never truly ends. Whether your collection consists of vintage vinyl records, rare coins, comic books, or even antique typewriters, the pursuit of these items can feel like an endless treasure hunt. And that's precisely the beauty of it.

Never-Ending Discovery

As a collector, you've likely already realized that there is always more to learn, more to discover, and more to find. Each new addition to your collection can open up a world of history, craft, or culture you didn't know existed. Collecting is a dynamic process; it evolves, shifts, and surprises you in ways you may never expect. It's like walking through an endless maze where every turn leads to a new door, and behind each door is something you didn't even know you were looking for.

You might think, "Once I complete this collection, I'll feel satisfied." But seasoned collectors know that the word "complete" is a mirage. There's always the next piece that complements the previous ones, a rare edition you hadn't heard of, or a discovery that reinvents the way you see your existing items. The thrill of the chase, the joy of unearthing something unique, and the satisfaction of giving that item a place in your curated world—this is the lifeblood of a collector.

It's not just about owning; it's about growing. Your knowledge, appreciation, and understanding deepen with each find. You might start off thinking you're just collecting things, but in reality, you're collecting stories, memories, and pieces of the world's vast history. A coin isn't just a coin, a comic book isn't just ink and paper—they are time capsules, portals to different eras, pieces of someone else's life that you now get to preserve.

Tips for Staying Passionate

As your collection grows, though, it's easy for the thrill to fade, for the passion to simmer down. Perhaps you feel like you've seen it all, or maybe the sheer number of items you own has made the pursuit feel overwhelming rather than exciting. It's natural for the honeymoon phase of any hobby to end—but there are ways to rekindle the flame and keep the fire of passion burning.

1. **Rotate Your Focus**: If you've spent years focused on collecting one type of item, say rare stamps, consider expanding or pivoting your interest. Maybe vintage postcards or old letters could add a new layer to your collection. Changing the lens through which you view your passion can reignite your curiosity.

2. **Embrace Community**: Collecting can be a solitary activity, but it doesn't have to be. Join a group, attend conventions, or engage in online forums. Sharing your finds and hearing others' stories will remind you why you fell in love with collecting in the first place. Nothing beats the camaraderie of talking to someone who "gets it."

3. **Research Beyond the Object**: Instead of simply seeking the next item to add to your shelves, dive deeper into the history and stories behind what you already own. Why was this object created? What was happening in the world at the time? The more you learn, the more appreciation you will gain. Sometimes, understanding the context can renew your sense of wonder.

4. **Set Challenges for Yourself**: If your collection feels stagnant, set new goals. Try to find a particularly rare item or challenge yourself to complete a themed sub-collection within a year. You could also create an exhibition of your collection, whether it's a small gathering for friends or an online showcase. The challenge will push you to see your collection with fresh eyes.

5. **Take Breaks When Needed**: It's important to remember that hobbies are meant to enrich your life, not burden it. If you feel your interest waning, don't be afraid to step away for a while. Sometimes, the

space you give yourself allows you to return with a renewed sense of excitement. Like a garden, your passion needs moments of rest to bloom again.

A Collector's Legacy

Perhaps one of the most meaningful aspects of collecting is the legacy you build along the way. Your collection tells a story—not just of the items themselves but of you as a person. What you choose to collect, how you care for those objects, and how you curate your collection all reflect your values, interests, and passions. Over time, this collection becomes more than just "things"—it becomes an extension of who you are, a time capsule of your life's journey.

Collectors, in many ways, are the custodians of history. Whether you realize it or not, you're preserving something for the future, ensuring that these items—and the stories they carry—are not forgotten. Even after you're gone, your collection may continue to inspire, intrigue, and bring joy to others, just as it did for you.

The Journey Continues

In the end, collecting is a lifelong journey. It's about discovery, passion, and connection—not only with the objects you gather but with the world around you. There will always be new items, new stories, and new lessons waiting to be uncovered. So, keep exploring, keep learning, and most importantly, keep collecting.

After all, the best part about being a collector is that there's always something more just around the corner. And who knows? Your next great find might be just one adventure away.